SAINSBURY'S

CURRIES

PAT CHAPMAN

ACKNOWLEDGEMENTS

Series Editor: **Nicola Hill**
Copy Editor: **Suzy Powling**
Art Direction: **Sara Kidd**
Designer: **Sue Storey**
Production Controller: **Janet Slater**
Photographer: **Paul Moon**
Home Economist: **Mandy Wagstaff**
Stylist: **Marian Price**
Jacket Photographer: **Vernon Morgan**
Jacket Home Economist: **Allyson Birch**
Jacket Stylist: **Lorrie Mack**

NOTES

1. Standard level spoon measurements are used in all recipes.
1 tablespoon = one 15 ml spoon
1 teaspoon = one 5 ml spoon

2. Both metric and imperial measurements have been given in all recipes. Use one set of measurements only and not a mixture of both.

3. Ovens should be preheated to the specified temperature – if using a fan assisted oven, follow manufacturer's instructions for adjusting the temperature.

4. Eggs should be size 3 unless otherwise stated.

5. Pepper should be freshly ground black pepper unless otherwise stated.

6. Milk should be full-fat unless otherwise stated.

7. Fresh herbs should be used unless otherwise stated. If unavailable use dried herbs as an alternative but halve the quantities stated.

8. All microwave information is based on a 650 watt oven. Follow manufacturer's instructions for an oven with a different wattage.

9. All ingredients marked with an asterisk refer to the glossary.

Published exclusively for
J Sainsbury plc
Stamford Street, London SE1 9LL
by Cathay Books, an imprint of Reed Consumer Books Limited
Michelin House, 81 Fulham Road, London SW3 6RB
and Auckland, Melbourne, Singapore and Toronto

First published 1989
Reprinted 1990, 1991, 1992, 1993

ISBN 0 86178 530 4

Produced by Mandarin Offset
Printed in Hong Kong

CONTENTS

INTRODUCTION

THIS SELECTION OF RECIPES INCLUDES RESTAURANT FAVOURITES, A NUMBER OF UNUSUAL DISHES AND SOME ORIGINAL CREATIONS. THE TECHNIQUES USED WILL HELP YOU ACHIEVE THE BEST FLAVOURS AND TEXTURES.

The title 'curries' has been taken in its widest sense, so that the recipes include an impressive variety of dishes – from starters to accompaniments. Such a selection will enable the cook to produce anything from a single snack to a complete curry banquet with ease, confidence and minimal time.

It is a book designed for both the novice and the seasoned experienced cook. Above all it sets out to dispel the reputation that curry is always hot and greasy. Heat can be added in the form of chilli* or pepper and how much you add is up to you. Try Chicken Korma (see page 62) or Baked Spicy Quail (see page 70) if you want to sample mild and subtle spicy cooking. And while it is true that Indian cooking uses a liberal quantity of oil during cooking, any excess should be removed before serving.

WHAT IS CURRY?

There are 15 languages used in different areas of India but the word 'curry' did not originate in any of them. In fact it was the English who coined the word when the first travellers reached India in the early 1600s. It probably derived from the Southern Indian Tamil word kari, which is a thin spicy sauce though it could equally be turkuri, a vegetable curry or stew which gave us the word kudhi (karhi or kadi) a Gujarati soup-like dish made with spices, and yogurt (see page 13). On the other hand it may have derived from the name of a leaf used in the making of curry powder (which the Indians call masalla) – kari phulia or curry leaves*; or from the word for the wok-like cooking utensil used everywhere in the subcontinent – the karahi. In traditional India this would be made from beaten or cast iron with a rounded bottom so that it can be embedded in a charcoal fire. Western versions have flattened bottoms to allow them to be used on electric rings and ceramic and gas hobs. Because of the karahi's rounded sides, heat is intense at the base and minimal at the sides, making for good control over stir-frying. A large flat frying pan can be used as an alternative, but this is not as effective.

KEEPING COOKED CURRY

The longer a curry is kept, the more its flavours develop. Its taste will change again after it has been frozen and reheated. This is because the spices in the curry are blending with the other ingredients, and the longer it is kept the more effective the process. Some people prefer a curry which has been allowed to mature, others prefer the fresher taste of a curry straight from the pot. In general the marination process seems to make curries taste less spicy, because the spices have been absorbed by the main ingredients and their strength dissipated. I prefer to overspice slightly if I know that I'm going to keep a curry. Alternatively it can be 'pepped-up' with a small amount of garam masala, aromatic salt or curry paste.

The rules for keeping any food for a period are always the same. After cooking, cool as quickly as possible, cover and refrigerate. Fish and shellfish should only be kept by freezing.

FREEZING

To freeze curry, undercook the dish slightly (by about 10 minutes in the case of meat). Let it cool, then remove any whole spices such as cinnamon stick, cassia bark*, cloves and cardamoms*, which are inclined to take on a slightly astringent taste after being frozen. Then place the curry in freezer bags or containers. Use within 3 months.

To reheat frozen curries, defrost completely and cook in a preheated oven, 190°C, 375°F, Gas Mark 5 for about 45 minutes. Alternatively defrost at room temperature or in a microwave on Defrost for 20–25 minutes, stirring once, then reheat on High Power for 8–10 minutes, stirring twice, for a 4 portion quantity.

SPICES

There is no standard curry and there are as many curries as there are cooks. Spices make the greatest contribution to this variety since there are over 60 to choose from. They can be ground or whole, roasted or fried, and added in any combination or order.

The cooking techniques resulting in what the early Englishmen called simply 'curry' had been in everyday use in India for thousands of years and remain unchanged to this day. In traditional Indian home cooking, spicing is treated very seriously. It involves some complicated rituals and time consuming preparation and cooking methods. I have endeavoured here to simplify the technique of spicing. I have followed the example of the restaurants by using curry bases such as Mild Curry Powder and Curry Purée, (see pages 7 and 9). The spice content can be varied to your taste. Most of the recipes require additional spicing, listed together, under the heading – spices.

WHAT DO SPICES DO?

Alone, spices are unpalatable but when used in cooking they impart both fragrance and flavour to the other ingredients. Some spices are used to give savoury tastes, some to give slightly sweet or aromatic tastes. Those chosen for their bitter flavour should be used in moderation (turmeric* and fenugreek seeds* for example). Certain spices can be chosen for the colour they give while others are just selected for texture (poppy and sesame seeds, for example). A few spices are used to give curries heat, (chilli* and pepper, for example).

USING SPICES

Spices are used whole or ground to give a totally different effect. Either way they must be cooked early in the preparation of the dish otherwise they retain a harsh, raw taste.

ROASTING SPICES

Where a recipe calls for spices to be roasted and sometimes ground afterwards, follow the instructions given for Garam Masala (see page 10).

FRYING WHOLE SPICES

Spices should be fried in hot oil, but it is crucial that they are not burnt. The process takes a maximum of 1 minute during which time the spices should be kept on the move by stir-frying.

GROUND SPICES

Recipes which specify ground spices refer to commercially ground spices. Every mixture of ground spices for use in Indian cooking is called in Hindi a *masala*, and in English, curry powder. The spices are never pre-roasted, but raw. They must be cooked, usually by frying. This can be done by adding them in dry form to hot oil, but as they are easily burnt, I prefer to blend the dry spices together, then add enough water to make a paste. Let the paste stand while the oil heats up to allow the powder to absorb the water, then fry. Follow the method for Mild Curry Paste (see page 8), using vinegar if you wish to bottle the cooked paste for long-term storage, and adjusting the quantity of oil according to the amount of spices.

BURNT SPICES

If you burn spices (including ginger and garlic) in the early preparation stages, discard them and start again, or your meal will taste of bitter carbon rather than subtle spicing.

MAKING CHUPPATI

FOR INGREDIENTS AND METHOD FOR MAKING CHUPPATI SEE RECIPE ON PAGE 92

Mixing the flour with enough water to make a soft pliable dough.

Rolling a piece of dough into a circle about 18–20 cm (7–8 inches) in diameter.

Cooking a chuppati in a dry frying pan over a fairly high heat. After 20–30 seconds the patches appear.

PREPARING PLAIN RICE

A QUICK AND FOOLPROOF METHOD OF PREPARING BASMATI RICE

It is difficult to predict individual appetites for rice. A modest serving would be 50 g (2 oz); 75 g (3 oz) is average and 125 g (4 oz) is generous

Pick through the rice to make sure it is free of grit. Leave it to soak in cold water for about 30 minutes. Bring about 1.5–2 litres (2½–3½ pints) of water to boil. Rinse the rice several times in cold water, and finally in hot water. Tip it into the boiling water and put on the lid.

After 1 minute, stir the rice. Replace the lid and continue cooking for 6 minutes. Taste the rice to see if it is ready. It should be almost cooked – simmer it for 1–2 minutes more.

Strain the rice well, shaking out all the excess water. Transfer to a serving dish and keep it warm until you are ready to serve, fluffing it up with a fork from time to time, to allow steam to escape.

Nutritional content per average serving: Carbohydrate: 65 g   Fibre: 2 g   Kilocalories: 270

Stirring the rice while cooking.

Straining the rice through a sieve.

Fluffing the cooked rice with a fork.

MILD CURRY POWDER

THERE ARE MANY GOOD COMMERCIALLY PREPARED CURRY POWDERS AVAILABLE BUT FOR THOSE WHO PREFER TO MAKE THEIR OWN I HAVE GIVEN THE BASIC RECIPE WHICH CAN BE USED FOR THE DISHES IN THIS BOOK. ADJUST THE QUANTITIES TO MAKE A SMALLER OR LARGER BATCH IF REQUIRED; THIS WILL KEEP FOR UP TO 18 MONTHS IN A LARGE JAR (IN THE DARK AND WITH A LID ON). FOR A VERY MILD POWDER, LEAVE OUT THE CHILLI*, MUSTARD AND PEPPER; FOR A MUCH HOTTER RESULT, INCREASE THESE 3 INGREDIENTS ACCORDING TO TASTE. THE QUANTITIES GIVEN ARE FOR GUIDANCE ONLY – IF YOU DO NOT HAVE SOME OF THE SMALLER QUANTITY ITEMS OMIT THEM OR USE THE SAME AMOUNT OF A MILD COMMERCIALLY PREPARED CURRY POWDER IN THEIR PLACE

Mix together the following:

GROUND SPICES	Heaped Teaspoons		Heaped Teaspoons		Heaped Teaspoons
coriander*	12	paprika	4	ground ginger	1
white cumin	6	turmeric*	4	mango powder* (optional)	1
gram flour* (optional)	5	garam masala	4	chilli powder*	1
garlic powder	5	curry leaves* (optional)	1	mustard powder	1
fenugreek seeds*	4	asafoetida* (optional)	1	white pepper	1

MAKES APPROXIMATELY 250 g (8 oz)

Nutritional content per quantity: Carbohydrate: 65 g   Fat: 27 g   Kilocalories: 585

MILD CURRY PASTE

It is useful to keep bottled curry paste in stock. There are a number of commercially made preparations available – use medium strength for the recipes in this book – but it is easy and quite rewarding to make it yourself

250 g (8 oz) Mild Curry Powder (see page 7)
250 ml (8 fl oz) vinegar
250 ml (8 fl oz) vegetable oil

Mix the curry powder with the vinegar and enough water to make a paste which is not too runny. Heat the oil in a large frying pan or wok. Add the paste: it will splutter at first but soon settle down. Stir-fry for 15 minutes or so until the water has completely evaporated to leave a creamy paste. The oil will rise to the surface when the paste is set aside. This means it is fully cooked. Transfer the slightly cooled paste to a warm sterilized bottle. Heat a little more oil and pour it on top of the paste to ensure no mould develops. Cover the bottle tightly with a lid. It will keep indefinitely providing all the water has evaporated.

MAKES APPROXIMATELY 425 g (14 oz)

Nutritional content per quantity: Carbohydrate: 65 g   Fat: 275 g   Kilocalories: 2830

QUICK CURRY PURÉE

This alternative method which can be used whenever curry purée is specified, is useful if you are in a hurry, as it is quick and easy to prepare. The texture however will not be the same

6 tablespoons concentrated butter or ghee*
2–4 cloves garlic, chopped finely
5 cm (2 inch) piece fresh root ginger, chopped finely
½ onion, chopped finely
2 teaspoons Mild Curry Paste (see above)
1 teaspoon tomato purée
1 tablespoon chopped coriander*

Heat the butter or ghee in a large frying pan or wok. Stir-fry the garlic for 1 minute. Add the ginger and stir-fry for 1 more minute. Add the onion and stir-fry for 2–3 more minutes. Mix in the curry paste, tomato purée and coriander with enough water to prevent the mixture from sticking. Simmer for 5 minutes. Use the purée immediately according to the individual recipe.

MAKES ENOUGH FOR A CURRY FOR 4

Nutritional content per quantity: Carbohydrate: 10 g   Fat: 95 g   Kilocalories: 900

AROMATIC SALT

Salt can be enhanced by mixing in spices and other ingredients. Spicy salt is commonly used in the Middle East and is delightful sprinkled over any food, including Indian

1 teaspoon coriander seeds*
1 teaspoon white cumin seeds
½ teaspoon szechuan pepper
½ teaspoon fennel seeds*
½ teaspoon allspice
½ teaspoon sesame seeds
6–8 hazelnuts
75 g (3 oz) sea salt

Roast the spices and the nuts as described for Garam Masala (see page 10). Let them cool and grind them with salt as finely or coarsely as you wish.

Transfer to an airtight jar (a small jam jar is ideal) and store in a cool, dry place. This will last indefinitely.

MAKES APPROXIMATELY 125 g (4 oz)

Nutritional content per quantity: Kilocalories: 250

CURRY PURÉE

IN INDIA FRESH GARLIC, GINGER, ONION, CORIANDER AND SPICES ARE 'WET GROUND' INTO A FINE PURÉE WHICH IS THEN FRIED AT THE BEGINNING OF MANY RECIPES. THIS IS USED TO GIVE A CREAMY TEXTURE AND SAVOURY TASTE TO CURRY DISHES. IT IS AN IMPORTANT COMPONENT IN THE MAKING OF A GOOD CURRY AND FEATURES IN MANY OF THE RECIPES IN THIS BOOK. IT IS USEFUL TO MAKE UP ONE LARGE BATCH AND FREEZE MOST OF IT. THIS IS A LARGE QUANTITY BUT THE TIME AND EFFORT SAVED MAKES IT WORTH DOING. THE QUANTITIES CAN BE SCALED DOWN AS REQUIRED

20 plump cloves garlic, peeled
250 g (8 oz) concentrated butter or ghee*
50 g (2 oz) piece fresh root ginger, chopped
5 onions, chopped coarsely
1 × 125–175 g (4–6 oz) bunch coriander*, chopped finely
250 g (8 oz) carrots, canned, frozen or pre-cooked fresh
900 g (2 lb) canned tomatoes
1 × 425 g (14 oz) can cream of tomato soup
7 heaped tablespoons Mild Curry Paste (see page 8)
salt

Place the garlic in a blender with a little water and process to a fine purée. Heat the butter or ghee in a 5.5 litre (10 pint) saucepan or use 2 smaller ones. Stir-fry the garlic purée for 5 minutes. Place the ginger in the blender (there is no need to rinse it between processes) with a little water and work to a fine purée. Add the ginger to the frying garlic and stir-fry for 5 more minutes.

Meanwhile purée the onions and coriander with a little water, working in batches and adding each one to the pan as it is ready. Cover the pan and continue to cook for 30 minutes over a gentle heat, stirring occasionally. Purée the carrots and tomatoes with their juices and add them to the pan. Cook the mixture for 5 minutes and add the tomato soup, curry paste and salt to taste. Simmer for a further 30 minutes. Add a little water if necessary to maintain a reasonably thick consistency.

Freezing: is recommended. Divide the purée equally into 14 containers, such as 450 g (14 oz) yogurt pots. Filled just over half way each one will hold about 300 ml (½ pint) of purée, the perfect amount for the average curry for 4. Place in the freezer; when solid, turn out and transfer to freezer bags to save space. Place in the freezer until needed.

MAKES APPROXIMATELY 4 LITRES (7 PINTS)

Nutritional content per 300 ml (½ pint):	Carbohydrate: 10 g	Fat: 22 g	Fibre: 2 g	Kilocalories: 240

Puréeing the garlic cloves with a little water in a blender until a fine purée is reached.

Cooking the garlic, ginger, onions and coriander in a frying pan over a gentle heat, stirring occasionally.

Simmering the curry purée mixture once the carrots, tomatoes, tomato soup, curry paste and salt have been added.

Tandoori masala

Tandoori masala is used in marinade mixtures and should be quite sour to taste. Combine all the spices well and transfer them to an airtight jar or tin. This quantity will mature with time, but should not be kept beyond 18 months. Alternatively use ready blended tandoori masala

GROUND SPICES	Heaped Teaspoons		Heaped Teaspoons		Heaped Teaspoons
coriander*	6	paprika	6	ground ginger	3
white cumin	6	garam masala	4	dried mint	3
garlic powder	6	mango powder* (optional)	3	chilli powder*	2

MAKES APPROXIMATELY 200 g (7 oz)

Nutritional content per quantity:	Carbohydrate: 50 g	Fat: 22 g	Kilocalories: 470

Tandoori paste

200 g (7 oz) Tandoori Masala (see above)
250 ml (8 fl oz) vinegar
250 ml (8 fl oz) vegetable oil

Mix the tandoori masala with the vinegar and enough water to make a paste. Heat the oil in a deep frying pan or wok. Add the paste: it will splutter at first but soon subside. Stir-fry for about 15 minutes until the liquid has evaporated to leave a creamy, smooth paste. Set the pan aside to cool. The oil will rise to the surface if the paste is fully cooked. Transfer the paste to a warm sterilized bottle and fill it to the top with a little more warm oil to prevent mould developing. Cover the bottle tightly and store in a cool dark place. It will keep indefinitely as long as all the liquid has evaporated.

MAKES APPROXIMATELY 375 g (12 oz)

Nutritional content per quantity:	Carbohydrate: 52 g	Fat: 271 g	Kilocalories: 2715

Garam masala

This is a mixture (*MASALA*) of hot (*GARAM*) and aromatic spices used as a condiment or as an ingredient added towards the end of the cooking time to perk up the spicing. This recipe is mild and fragrant, it can be made hotter by adding 1–6 teaspoons of pepper. There are many ready prepared blends of garam masala available, which can be used as an alternative

WHOLE SPICES
50 g (2 oz) coriander seeds*
50 g (2 oz) white cumin seeds
25 g (1 oz) cinnamon stick or cassia bark *
25 g (1 oz) fennel seeds*
10 g (¼ oz) whole cloves
10 g (¼ oz) brown or black cardamoms*
10 g (¼ oz) green cardamoms*
10 g (¼ oz) nutmeg

Roasting can be done in the oven, under the grill or in a dry frying pan on the hob. Spread the spices flat in a single layer in a baking tin, or grill pan. Place in a preheated oven, 160°C, 325°F, Gas Mark 3, for 10 minutes, or under a preheated grill at the half-way point for about 6 minutes, stirring once or twice, or on the stove, stir-frying for 5 minutes. Leave the spices to cool. Grind them in a coffee grinder, the spice mill attachment of a blender or by hand with a pestle and mortar. Transfer to an airtight jar and store in a cool dark place.

MAKES APPROXIMATELY 200 g (7 oz)

Nutritional content per quantity:	Carbohydrate: 71 g	Fat: 40 g	Kilocalories: 700

GLOSSARY

Asafoetida:
This pale yellow spice originates as the gum or sap of a tree. It crystallizes and is then ground to a powder. It has a strong smell and is used in lentil or bean dishes.

Ata or atta flour:
Finely ground from a hard wheat, this wholemeal flour is used to make many Indian breads, such as chuppati. British wholemeal flour is from softer wheat but can be used as a substitute.

Barbery (Zereshk):
These are small, wrinkly, dark brown soft berries, resembling raisins. They are very sour and are used in Persian spicy cooking.

Brinjal pickle:
Aubergines pickled in a spicy, curry sauce. A favourite condiment in India.

Cardamom (Elaichi):
Green or white; small pods with a delicate very aromatic taste. Brown or black; much larger than the green and slightly more pungent, though still aromatic. Used in garam masala.

Cassia bark:
This is the bark of a type of cinnamon tree. It is thicker than true cinnamon, but thicker cinnamon sticks can be used as an alternative. It has an aromatic, sweet fragrance and is used whole in certain dishes. It should be removed before serving as should cinnamon stick. It is also used ground in garam masala.

Chillies:
Fresh green and red; the green is slightly larger than the red, these are used to add heat to a dish. Prepare with care – do not touch your face or rub your eyes while handling them. Wash your hands after use. Dried whole red; again very hot especially the smaller ones, handle with the same care as fresh chillies. Chilli powder is made from ground red chillies and is used to add heat.

Chinese five spice powder:
One of the few spices used in Chinese cookery, this is a fragrant combination of equal amounts of cassia bark, cloves, fennel, star anise and Szechuan pepper, usually ground, sometimes whole. It is best to roast and grind it oneself to get the freshest taste. Can be used in place of garam masala and vice versa.

Coconut:
Fresh coconut is widely used in the curry lands. When buying, choose one which sounds like it has plenty of liquid (coconut milk) inside. Drain this off by making holes in 2 of the 3 'eyes'. Bake for 15 minutes in a preheated oven 160°C, 325°F, Gas

Mark 3. Crack open and scrape out the flesh. Grind the flesh in a food processor or coffee grinder. Substitutes are desiccated coconut or coconut powder. The latter is finely ground coconut flesh which, when mixed with milk or water becomes a creamy tasty paste. Creamed coconut is available in a block. It must be melted in a liquid base as on its own it burns. It melts more easily if chopped coarsely.

Coriander:
Of special importance in curry cooking, and used in two forms. The fresh leaves (Hara Dhania) give a distinctive fragrant taste when added towards the end of cooking or as a garnish. The seeds (Dhania) of the plant which are greyish brown in colour are the spice most prolifically used in curry cooking and are available whole or ground.

Curry leaves (Kari phulla):
Aromatic leaves of the Neem tree, these green leaves are available dried. They give a lemony taste and are used in curry powder and lime rice.

Fennel (Soonf):
These aniseed-flavoured seeds are yellowy green in colour and are used in garam masala.

Fenugreek (Methi):
Available dried as a dark green leaf with a savoury taste, and in the form of yellow seeds which are savoury tasting but bitter and therefore should be used with care. These are used in curry powder.

Fish sauce:
Available in bottles, this very salty, thin, brown liquid is made by fermenting anchovies with salt and soy and draining off the liquid.

Ghee:
A clarified butter which makes a good cooking fat as it can be heated to a high temperature without burning. Concentrated butter or vegetable oil make good alternatives but ordinary butter does not as it burns.

Gram flour:
A flour made from lentils and used to thicken sauces, in curry powder and to make Pakoras. Finely milled to a light gold colour, it has a distinctive taste. Make your own substitute by finely grinding yellow split peas.

Koo-koo sabzi:
A mixture of fresh or dried herbs used in Persian cooking, including chives, parsley, spring onion and dill.

Lime leaves:
A delicate flavouring agent used in Thai cooking. The oval leaves are deep green, a little larger than bay leaves and have a

sweet, enticing taste. Available fresh, but more often dried, they are also called 'makrut', citrus leaf or kaffir lime leaves.

Mango powder:
The ground powder of dried mangoes. This is sour and should be used sparingly.

Mustard blend oil:
The oil from black mustard seeds, this is quite pungent and should not be consumed in its pure form. Blended with vegetable oil it has a sweet taste.

Mustard seeds (Rai):
Small brown seeds. These are quite hot and are popular in Southern India.

Panch phoran:
A mixture of five whole spices used in Bengali vegetable cooking. The most commonly used mixture is equal parts of the seeds of white cumin, fennel, fenugreek, mustard and wild onion.

Prawn ballichow:
This is made from prawns and used as a relish or as a cooking ingredient in South India, Burma and Thailand.

Saffron (Zafran):
The deep orange stigma of a crocus, available in strands or as a powder. It gives a yellow colour and a subtle flavour.

Shrimp paste:
Used with discrimination to create a background taste in meat, poultry and vegetable dishes in Thailand (where it is called *kapi*), Burma (*nga-pi*) and Malaysia (*blachan*). It is prepared in a compressed rectangular block. Although shrimp paste does not go off, make sure it is well cooked in the dish in which it is being used. Shrimp powder is a substitute.

Star anise:
An eight pointed star shaped, brown, very attractive spice.

Tamarind:
A fleshy fruit resembling a long date. It tastes sour and supplies a distinctive taste to the cooking of South India. It is normally available in compressed blocks which are quite dry and do not deteriorate. To use, cut off part of the block; add it to 4 times its volume of water in a small pan. Bring the water to simmering point. Cool and push the pulp through a sieve to give a thick liquid. Discard the pulp. Lemon juice or vinegar can be used as alternatives.

Turmeric:
Used in powdered form this is the ground root of the turmeric plant. It is a natural combining agent which gives curry its customary yellow colour.

Wild onion seeds: (Kalonji):
These are black irregular tiny nugget shaped seeds which are aromatic in flavour once cooked.

SOUPS, STARTERS AND LIGHT MEALS

A SELECTION OF DELICIOUS TRADITIONAL INDIAN AND INDIAN-INSPIRED RECIPES TO SUIT EVERY POSSIBLE OCCASION FROM FAMILY MEALS TO ENTERTAINING, RANGING FROM THE FIERY HOT MULLIGATAWNY SOUP TO THE MILDER CHICKEN SHASHLIK KEBAB, THERE IS SURE TO BE SOMETHING TO SUIT EVERY TASTE.

MULLIGATAWNY

2 tablespoons sunflower oil
1 clove garlic, chopped finely
1 onion, chopped
2 or more green chillies*, chopped finely
900 ml (1 ½ pints) vegetable stock or
    water
1 tablespoon red lentils
1 tablespoon Basmati rice
1 small carrot, shredded
3–4 tablespoons lemon juice, strained
salt
SPICES:
2 teaspoons Mild Curry Powder (see
    page 7)
1 teaspoon celery seeds
1 teaspoon black mustard seeds*
1 teaspoon black peppercorns

Heat the oil in a 2.5 litre (4 pint) saucepan. Add the spices and stir-fry for 1 minute. Add the garlic and onion and stir-fry for 2 more minutes. Add all the remaining ingredients. Bring to the boil and simmer for 10–15 minutes. Serve very hot.

Freezing: is recommended. When cold store and freeze in a foil or rigid plastic container. This will keep for up to 3 months. To serve, turn into a pan and heat gently until defrosted. Bring to the boil and simmer for 10 minutes, or cover and microwave on Defrost for 20–25 minutes, stirring once, then reheat on High Power for 8–10 minutes, stirring twice.

Microwave: Place the oil in a large heatproof bowl and cook on High Power for 2 minutes. Add the spices and cook on High Power for 2 minutes. Add the garlic and onion, cover and cook on High Power for 2 minutes. Add the chillies, stock, lentils, rice, carrot, lemon juice and salt. Cover and cook on High Power for 15–20 minutes, stirring twice until cooked. Serve very hot.

SERVES 4

Nutritional content per serving: Carbohydrate: 12 g   Fat: 8 g   Fibre: 2 g   Kilocalories: 130

KARHI

KARHI, PRONOUNCED 'CURRY', IS A YOGURT-BASED SOUP, MADE AS THICK OR THIN AS YOU CHOOSE. IT IS GOOD HOT OR COLD

300 ml (½ pint) natural yogurt
2 tablespoons gram flour* or cornflour
1 tablespoon desiccated coconut or
    coconut powder*
2 tablespoons sunflower oil
600 ml (1 pint) vegetable stock or water
1 tablespoon white sugar
salt
coriander* or parsley sprigs to garnish
SPICES:
1 teaspoon black mustard seeds*
½ teaspoon white cumin seeds
6 dried curry leaves* (optional)
2 teaspoons Mild Curry Powder (see
    page 7)
pinch of asafoetida* (optional)
chilli powder* to taste

Beat together the yogurt, gram flour or cornflour and coconut to make a smooth paste. Heat the oil in a 2.5 litre (4 pint) saucepan. Add the spices and stir-fry for 1 minute.

Take the pan off the heat to cool a little then add the stock or water, sugar and salt to taste and simmer for 20 minutes. Pour the soup into bowls and garnish with coriander or parsley. If serving cold, allow to cool completely before pouring into bowls and garnishing.

Freezing: is recommended. When cold, store and freeze in a foil or plastic container. This will keep for up to 3 months. Leave to defrost at room temperature, then transfer to a pan and slowly bring to the boil, stirring. Lower the heat and simmer for 10–15 minutes or cover and microwave on Defrost for 20–25 minutes, stirring once, then reheat on High Power, for 8–10 minutes, stirring twice.

SERVES 4

Nutritional content per serving: Carbohydrate: 10 g   Fat: 14 g   Fibre: 2 g   Kilocalories: 185

Mulligatawny; Karhi

CHICKEN CHAT

USE 125 G (4 OZ) DRIED CHICK PEAS WHICH HAVE BEEN SOAKED AND COOKED INSTEAD OF THE CAN

250 g (8 oz) boneless, skinless chicken
  breast
3–4 tablespoons lemon juice
2 tablespoons vegetable oil
1 onion, sliced
2 teaspoons Mild Curry Powder or Paste
  (see pages 7 or 8)
1 tablespoon tomato purée
4 small tomatoes, skinned and quartered
1 tablespoon vinegar
1 teaspoon dried mint
1 × 425 g (15 oz) can chick peas
1 tablespoon chopped coriander*
salt
coriander sprigs to garnish
SPICES:
1 teaspoon white cumin seeds
1 teaspoon black mustard seeds*
1/2 teaspoon fenugreek seeds*

Cut the chicken into 5 cm × 5 mm (2 × 1/4 inch) strips and rub with lemon juice. Leave to marinate for 1–2 hours. Heat the oil in a large frying pan or wok and stir-fry the chicken for 5 minutes until it goes white. Remove the chicken and set aside. Place the large frying pan or wok over a moderate heat and fry the onion until soft and transparent. Add the spices and stir-fry for 1 minute. Add the curry powder or paste, tomato purée, tomatoes, vinegar and enough water to prevent them sticking to the pan. Stir-fry for 3–5 minutes then add the mint, chicken, chick peas and coriander. Season with salt. Cook until heated through. Garnish with coriander.

Freezing: is recommended. When cold, freeze in an earthenware dish. This will keep for up to 3 months. Defrost at room temperature for 6–8 hours to serve cold. To serve hot, reheat in a covered dish in a preheated oven 180°C, 350°F, Gas Mark 4 for 45 minutes or cover and microwave on Defrost for 20–25 minutes, stirring once, then reheat on High Power for 8–10 minutes, stirring twice.

SERVES 4

Nutritional content per serving:	Carbohydrate: 20 g	Fat: 14 g	Fibre: 6 g	Kilocalories: 295

ALOO CHAT

500 g (1 lb) potatoes
2 tablespoons vegetable or mustard blend
  oil*
1 onion, sliced
2 teaspoons Mild Curry Powder or Paste
  (see pages 7 or 8)
1 tablespoon tomato purée
4 small tomatoes, quartered
1 tablespoon vinegar
1 teaspoon dried mint
1 tablespoon chopped coriander*
salt
SPICES:
1 teaspoon white cumin seeds
1 teaspoon black mustard seeds*
1/2 teaspoon fenugreek seeds*

Peel and dice the potatoes if they are large. If they are small and new leave whole with the skins on. Boil them until they are almost cooked, strain and set aside. Heat the oil in a large frying pan or wok and stir-fry the onion until soft and transparent. Add the spices and stir-fry for 1 minute. Add the curry powder or paste, tomato purée, tomatoes, vinegar and enough water to prevent them from sticking to the pan. Stir-fry for 3–5 minutes then add the mint, potatoes and coriander. Season with salt to taste. Serve hot or cold, with a salad.

Freezing: is recommended. When cold, freeze in an earthenware dish. This will keep for up to 3 months. Defrost at room temperature for 6–8 hours to serve cold. To serve hot, reheat in a covered dish in a preheated oven 180°C, 350°F, Gas Mark 4 for 45 minutes or cover and microwave on Defrost for 20–25 minutes, stirring once, then reheat on High Power for 8–10 minutes, stirring twice.

SERVES 4

Nutritional content per serving:	Carbohydrate: 31 g	Fat: 10 g	Fibre: 2 g	Kilocalories: 225

Chicken Chat; Channa Chat; Aloo Chat

CHANNA CHAT

250 g (8 oz) chick peas
2 tablespoons vegetable oil
1 onion, sliced
2 teaspoons Mild Curry Paste (see page 8)
1 tablespoon tomato purée
4 small tomatoes, quartered
1 tablespoon vinegar
1 teaspoon dried mint
1 tablespoon chopped coriander*
salt
mint sprigs to garnish
SPICES:
1 teaspoon white cumin seeds
1 teaspoon black mustard seeds*
½ teaspoon fenugreek seeds*

Carefully pick over the chick peas to remove any grit. Soak them overnight in a large pan with 1.25 litres (2 pints) water. Rinse the chick peas and return them to the pan with 1.25 litres (2 pints) of fresh water. Bring to the boil and cook for 45 minutes until cooked but not mushy. Strain and set aside. Heat the oil in a large frying pan or wok and fry the onion until soft and transparent. Add the spices and stir-fry them for 1 minute. Add the curry paste, tomato purée, tomatoes, vinegar and enough water to prevent them from sticking to the pan. Stir-fry for 3–5 minutes then add the mint, coriander and chick peas and salt to taste. Garnish with mint and serve hot or cold with a salad.

SERVES 4

Nutritional content per serving: Carbohydrate: 35 g   Fat: 13 g   Fibre: 10 g   Kilocalories: 305

CURRIED PRAWN COCKTAIL

THIS IS A VARIATION ON A FAVOURITE BRITISH STARTER AND IS VERY EASY TO MAKE. THE CREAM MAY BE OMITTED BY HEALTH-CONSCIOUS DINERS – SIMPLY DOUBLE THE QUANTITY OF YOGURT

2 tablespoons natural yogurt
2 tablespoons double cream
2 teaspoons Tandoori Paste (see page 10)
1 teaspoon Mild Curry Paste (see page 8)
500 g (1 lb) tiny fresh shrimps, or prawns
½ small iceberg lettuce, shredded finely
TO GARNISH:
lemon or lime slices
parsley sprigs
red pepper strips

Mix the yogurt with the cream, tandoori paste and curry paste. Fold in the shrimps or prawns.

Place the lettuce at the base of 4 stemmed glasses. Spoon the shrimp mixture carefully on top. Garnish each glass with a slice of lemon or lime, parsley sprigs and strips of red pepper to serve.

SERVES 4

Nutritional content per serving: Carbohydrate: 2 g   Fat: 7 g   Fibre: 1 g   Kilocalories: 150

AVOCADO CURRIED CRAB

SIMPLE TO MAKE AND AN EFFECTIVE STARTER, THE CURRIED CRAB IS BASED ON A RECIPE FROM GOA AND CAN BE SERVED HOT OR COLD. THE CRAB, CREAM AND PASTE MIXTURE CAN BE PREPARED IN ADVANCE AND REFRIGERATED FOR 3–4 HOURS UNTIL REQUIRED

75 g (3 oz) white crab meat, shredded
75 g (3 oz) brown crab meat, shredded
2 tablespoons double cream
2–4 tablespoons Tandoori Paste (see page 10)
2 ripe avocados
parsley sprigs to garnish

Combine all the crab meat with the cream and tandoori paste.

Just before serving, cut the avocados in half and remove the stones. Spoon the crab mixture into the cavity of the avocados and build it up over the surface.

Place parsley sprigs on each avocado half to garnish. Serve immediately with a salad.

SERVES 4

Nutritional content per serving: Carbohydrate: 2 g   Fat: 26 g   Fibre: 2 g   Kilocalories: 290

SPICED SCAMPI BITES

BREADED FROZEN SCAMPI PIECES ARE SPICED AND THEN DEEP-FRIED

2 eggs, beaten
1 tablespoon Mild Curry Paste (see page 8)
500 g (1 lb) frozen breaded scampi, defrosted
50 g (2 oz) fresh breadcrumbs
vegetable oil for deep-frying
2 teaspoons Garam Masala (see page 10)

Mix together the eggs and curry paste. Roll the scampi in this mixture then roll them in breadcrumbs.

Heat the oil to 190°C, 375°F or until a cube of bread browns in 30 seconds. Deep-fry the scampi for 5 minutes, or shallow-fry until golden. Remove from the pan and sprinkle with garam masala. Serve on a bed of salad.

SERVES 4

Nutritional content per serving: Carbohydrate: 36 g   Fat: 26 g   Fibre: 2 g   Kilocalories: 450

Curried Prawn Cocktail; Avocado Curried Crab; Spiced Scampi Bites

CHICKEN SHASHLIK KEBAB

500 g (1 lb) boned, skinned chicken breast
  cut into 16 × 3.5 cm (1½ inch) cubes
8 diamond-shaped pieces red pepper
8 diamond-shaped pieces green pepper
8 diamond-shaped pieces yellow pepper
8 diamond-shaped pieces raw onion
4 green chillies* (optional)
1 lemon or lime, cut into quarters
MARINADE:
3 tablespoons sunflower oil
2 teaspoons garlic purée
1 tablespoon Mild Curry Paste (see page 8)
2 tablespoons natural yogurt
TO GARNISH:
parsley sprigs
cucumber fans

Beat the marinade ingredients into a paste. Immerse the chicken in the paste, cover and refrigerate for at least 6 hours, or a maximum of 30 hours. To cook the chicken, either braise the pieces in a preheated oven, 160°C, 325°F, Gas Mark 3, for 15–20 minutes, or grill, barbecue or stir-fry for the same time.

To serve, thread on to 25 cm (10 inch) bamboo skewers (using tongs) alternate pieces of chicken, peppers and onion, with a chilli if using, and cucumber fans, and a wedge of lemon or lime. Serve hot; re-heat briefly under the grill if necessary. Garnish with parsley sprigs and serve with a salad.

Microwave: Marinate the chicken pieces as above then thread onto bamboo skewers, alternating with the pieces of pepper, onion and chillies, if using. Place on a plate and cook on High Power for 5–6 minutes, rearranging halfway through cooking. Serve as above.

SERVES 4

Nutritional content per serving:	Carbohydrate: 3 g	Fat: 13 g	Fibre: 1 g	Kilocalories: 260

Chicken Shashlik Kebab

Beef Hasina Kebab

BEEF OR LAMB HASINA KEBAB

500 g (1 lb) extra lean beef or lamb, cut into 16 × 3.5 cm (1½ inch) cubes
8 diamond shaped pieces red pepper
8 diamond shaped pieces green pepper
8 diamond shaped pieces yellow pepper
8 diamond shaped pieces raw onion
1 lime or lemon, cut into quarters
4 green chillies* (optional)

MARINADE:
3 tablespoons sunflower or mustard blend oil*
2 teaspoons garlic purée
1 tablespoons Tandoori Paste (see page 10)
2 tablespoons natural yogurt

Beat the marinade ingredients into a paste. Immerse the beef or lamb pieces in the paste, cover and refrigerate for at least 6 hours, or a maximum of 30 hours.

To cook the beef or lamb either braise in a preheated oven, 160°C, 325°F, Gas Mark 3, for 30–40 minutes, depending on the cut of meat chosen, until tender, or grill, barbecue or stir-fry for the same time.

To serve, using tongs, thread alternate pieces of beef or lamb, peppers, onion, a lime or lemon wedge and a chilli, if using, on to 25 cm (10 inch) bamboo skewers. Serve hot; reheat briefly under the grill if necessary.

SERVES 4

Nutritional content per serving: Carbohydrate: 4 g   Fat: 20 g   Fibre: 1 g   Kilocalories: 350

PAKORA

THE PAKORA, ALSO KNOWN AS THE BHAJIA IN CERTAIN AREAS, IS A DEEP-FRIED FRITTER MADE USING GRAM FLOUR* AND A 'FILLING' OF YOUR CHOICE. HERE I HAVE USED SLICED ONION

125 g (4 oz) gram flour* or finely ground
   yellow split peas
1 tablespoon natural yogurt
2 tablespoons vinegar
1 clove garlic, chopped finely
1 onion, sliced thinly
1 tablespoon chopped coriander leaves*
½ teaspoon Aromatic Salt (see page 8)
vegetable oil for deep-frying
SPICES:
1 teaspoon white cumin seeds
1 teaspoon Garam Masala (see page 10)
1 tablespoon Mild Curry Paste (see page 8)
TO GARNISH:
Garam Masala
parsley sprigs

Mix together the flour, yogurt and vinegar with just enough water to make a thick paste. Let it stand for 10 minutes before adding the remaining ingredients (except the oil) and the spices. Mix well.

Heat the oil to 190°C, 375°F. To test put 1 teaspoon of batter in the pan. It will splutter but float more or less at once. To make the pakoras, scoop out one eighth of the mixture on a tablespoon and place it carefully in the oil. Repeat this procedure 7 times, allowing a few seconds for the oil temperature to rise between each immersion. Fry the pakoras for 10 minutes, turning them once. Remove them from the oil with a slotted spoon and pat with kitchen paper to remove excess oil. Sprinkle with garam masala, and garnish with parsley sprigs. Serve hot with salad and a selection of chutneys.

Freezing: is recommended. When cold store and freeze in an earthenware dish, foil or plastic container. These will keep for up to 3 months. Reheat in a covered dish in a preheated oven 180°C, 350°C, Gas Mark 4 for 45 minutes.

SERVES 4

Nutritional content per serving:	Carbohydrate: 22 g	Fat: 13 g	Fibre: 5 g	Kilocalories: 235

VEGETABLE KEBAB

THESE ARE BREADCRUMBED RISSOLES WHICH ARE DEEP FRIED OR BAKED AND CAN BE SERVED ON THEIR OWN OR WITH CHUTNEYS

500 g (1 lb) mashed potato
125 g (4 oz) cooked peas
1 tablespoon plain or gram flour*
1 tablespoon desiccated coconut or
   coconut powder*
1 tablespoon Mild Curry Powder (see
   page 7)
½ teaspoon salt
1 egg, beaten
50 g (2 oz) dried breadcrumbs
vegetable oil for frying

Mix the potato and peas with the flour, coconut, curry powder and salt. Divide the mixture into 8 and form them into balls, rissoles or sausage shapes. Coat the kebabs with beaten egg and roll them in the breadcrumbs. Either shallow-fry or deep-fry until golden and hot (about 5 minutes). Serve with salad and a selection of chutneys.

Freezing: is recommended before frying the kebabs. Place the uncooked kebabs in a single layer on a tray and open-freeze. When frozen, store and freeze in a polythene bag. These will keep for up to 3 months. These can be fried from frozen, there is no need to defrost them.

SERVES 4

Nutritional content per serving:	Carbohydrate: 36 g	Fat: 24 g	Fibre: 8 g	Kilocalories: 380

Pakora; Vegetable Kebab

STUFFED TOMATOES AND STUFFED MUSHROOMS

ANY VEGETABLE WHICH HAS A CUP SHAPE MAKES AN IDEAL CASE FOR SPICY FILLINGS. FOR ATTRACTIVE STARTERS, CHOOSE CHERRY TOMATOES OR SMALL BUTTON MUSHROOMS. FOR A MAIN COURSE, YOU CAN USE EXTRA LARGE TOMATOES AND LARGER MUSHROOMS. RED, GREEN OR YELLOW PEPPERS OR BAKED POTATOES ARE ALSO PERFECT FOR STUFFING. THIS RECIPE MAKES ENOUGH FILLING FOR 24 SMALL MUSHROOMS OR 8 LARGE ONES; 12 CHERRY TOMATOES, 8 MEDIUM OR 4 EXTRA LARGE ONES OR 4 PEPPERS

1 × 284 g (10 oz) can diced mixed
 vegetables
250 g (8 oz) mashed potato
1 tablespoon Mild Curry Paste (see page 8)
1 teaspoon Garam Masala (see page 10)
1 tablespoon plain or gram flour*
½ teaspoon salt

Strain the can of vegetables and mash lightly. Mix with the other ingredients. Use this mixture to fill the vegetables of your choice – mushrooms, tomatoes or peppers – and place them on a baking sheet. Cover with foil and bake in a preheated oven 160°C, 325°F, Gas Mark 3 for 10–15 minutes. Serve hot.

Microwave: Prepare the stuffing as above and use to stuff either 4 large flat mushrooms or extra large tomatoes. Place in a dish, cover and cook on High Power for 4–6 minutes, until the filling is hot and the mushrooms or tomatoes are cooked. Serve hot.

SERVES 4

Nutritional content per serving: (stuffing)   Carbohydrate: 21 g   Fibre: 4 g   Kilocalories: 95

Stuffed Mushrooms and Stuffed Tomatoes

Vol-au-Vents

VOL-AU-VENTS

THE CURRY PUFF WAS INVENTED AT THE TIME OF THE RAJ AND CONSISTS OF A PUFF PASTRY CASE FILLED WITH A MINCED MEAT OR VEGETABLE CURRY. THIS ALTERNATIVE USES READY-MADE OR HOME-MADE VOL-AU-VENT CASES

Suggested fillings include the stuffing for Stuffed Mushrooms or Tomatoes (see left), Avocado Curried Crab (see page 17), Curried Prawn Cocktail (see page 17), Keema (see page 46) or Sag Bhajee (see page 78)

Fill the vol-au-vent cases with the filling of your choice. Place in a preheated oven, 160°C, 325°F, Gas Mark 3 for 10–15 minutes. Do not let the vol-au-vents stand after filling and before heating, or they may become soggy. They are best served hot or warm.

SERVES 4

Nutritional content per serving: Carbohydrate: 49 g   Fat: 24 g   Fibre: 5 g   Kilocalories: 435

FISH AND SEAFOOD DISHES

HUNDREDS OF DIFFERENT SPECIES OF FISH AND SHELLFISH THRIVE IN THE RIVERS AND OFF THE COASTS OF INDIA. THIS CHAPTER CONTAINS SOME DELICIOUS RECIPES FOR YOU TO EXPERIMENT WITH AND SHOWS HOW WELL FISH, SEAFOOD AND SPICES COMPLEMENT EACH OTHER.

JEERA PRAWN

WHITE CUMIN SEED (JEERA) IS THE PREDOMINANT SPICE IN THIS MOUTHWATERING DISH

4 tablespoons sunflower or mustard blend oil*
1 onion, chopped finely
¼ green pepper, chopped
2 tomatoes, skinned and chopped
1 green chilli* chopped finely
750 g (1½ lb) shelled prawns, defrosted if frozen
salt
fennel sprigs to garnish
SPICES:
2 tablespoons white cumin seeds
1 teaspoon turmeric*

Heat the oil in a frying pan until it is hot. Stir-fry the spices for 30 seconds. Add the onion and stir-fry until it starts to crisp (about 5 minutes). Add the pepper, tomatoes, chilli and salt to taste, and stir-fry for 2 more minutes.

Reduce the heat and add the prawns. Simmer for just long enough to make them hot (about 5 minutes). Do not overcook the prawns or they will become rubbery. Serve at once, garnished with fennel sprigs.

Microwave: Place the oil in a heatproof dish and cook on High Power for 2 minutes. Add the spices and cook on High Power for 2 minutes, stirring once. Add the onion and cook on High Power for 4 minutes, stirring once. Add the pepper, tomatoes and chilli and cook on High Power for 2 minutes. Add the prawns and cook on High Power for 4–6 minutes, stirring twice, until just cooked. Serve as above.

SERVES 4

Nutritional content per serving:	Carbohydrate: 8 g	Fat: 18 g	Fibre: 1 g	Kilocalories: 335

MEDITERRANEAN PRAWNS

THE LARGER THE MEDITERRANEAN PRAWNS THE BETTER FOR THIS BANGLADESHI RECIPE

8 large Mediterranean prawns, about 125 g (4 oz) each or 16 smaller Mediterranean prawns, 50 g (2 oz) each
3 tablespoons concentrated butter or ghee*
150 ml (¼ pint) Curry Purée (see page 9)
2 tablespoons Mild Curry Paste (see page 8)
2 tablespoons desiccated coconut or coconut powder*
1 tablespoon chopped coriander*
TO GARNISH:
3 teaspoons whole white cumin seeds, roasted
parsley sprigs

Carefully remove the heads, shells and tails from the prawns and cut away the veins. Wash the prawns well and drain them thoroughly.

Heat the butter or ghee in a large frying pan or wok. Stir-fry the curry purée for about 5 minutes. Add the curry paste. When the mixture is bubbling add the coconut, coriander and enough water to give a thick pouring consistency. Bring the sauce to the boil and place the prawns in the pan.

Reduce the heat to moderate and stir-fry for 15 minutes until the prawns are cooked through. Garnish with whole cumin seeds and parsley sprigs and serve immediately.

SERVES 4

Nutritional content per serving:	Carbohydrate: 4 g	Fat: 28 g	Fibre: 2 g	Kilocalories: 225

Mediterranean Prawns; Jeera Prawn

SOUTH INDIAN SPICED WHITEBAIT

2 tablespoons oil
2 cloves garlic, chopped finely
1 onion, sliced
2 teaspoons white sugar
1 tablespoon desiccated coconut or
　coconut powder*
1 teaspoon Worcestershire sauce
375 g (12 oz) whitebait, fresh or frozen
2 teaspoons Garam Masala (see page 10)
1 teaspoon chilli powder* (optional)
salt
vegetable oil for deep-frying
chopped parsley to garnish
SPICES:
1 teaspoon ground coriander*
1 teaspoon ground cumin
½ teaspoon turmeric*

A spicy deep-fried dish, quick and simple to make. If you are using frozen whitebait, defrost them sufficiently so that they can be easily separated. Heat the oil in a frying pan or wok and stir-fry the garlic for 1 minute. Add the onion and continue to stir-fry for 2–3 minutes. Add the spices, sugar and salt to taste and stir-fry for 2 more minutes. Add the coconut, Worcestershire sauce and enough water to prevent the mixture sticking to the pan. Set it aside while cooking the fish.

Heat the oil for deep-frying to 190°C, 375°F or until a cube of bread browns in 30 seconds. Place the whitebait in one at a time, otherwise they are likely to stick together. Fry them until they are crisp (about 5 minutes). Lift them out of the oil with a slotted spoon and strain to remove excess oil. Place the crispy whitebait into the spicy sauce. Place the frying pan over a moderate heat and stir-fry to ensure the sauce and fish are heated through and the fish nicely coated but still fairly dry. Sprinkle on the garam masala, chilli powder if using and salt to taste. Serve at once, garnished with chopped parsley.

SERVES 4 as a starter

Nutritional content per serving:　　Carbohydrate: 6 g　　Fat: 12 g　　Fibre: 2 g　　Kilocalories: 220

TANDOORI SARDINE

8 sardines, about 50 g (2 oz) each
lime wedges to garnish
TANDOORI MARINADE:
75 ml (3 fl oz) natural yogurt
75 ml (3 fl oz) milk
2 tablespoons Tandoori Masala (see page 10)
1 tablespoon Mild Curry Powder or Paste
　(see pages 7 or 8)
2 teaspoons Garam Masala (see page 10)
½–4 teaspoons chilli powder* (optional)
1 tablespoon chopped mint
1 tablespoon chopped coriander*
2 teaspoons garlic purée
2.5 cm (1 inch) piece fresh root ginger,
　chopped finely
1 teaspoon white cumin seeds, roasted and
　ground
2 tablespoons lemon juice

Combine all the marinade ingredients thoroughly in a large bowl. Clean the fish, keeping them whole. Coat them in the marinade and leave them covered in a cool place for 2–4 hours to absorb the flavours.

Bake the sardines in a preheated oven, 160°C, 325°F, Gas Mark 3 for 30 minutes until they are crusty. Alternatively grill or barbecue them. Do not set the rack too close to the heat and check after 20 minutes to ensure they are not burning. Garnish with lime wedges and serve with a salad and a selection of chutneys.

Microwave: Prepare the marinade as above and marinate the sardines. Place in a shallow cooking dish and cook on High Power for 4–5 minutes, or until the sardines are cooked. Quickly brown under a preheated hot grill until crusty and golden. Serve as above.

SERVES 4

Nutritional content per serving:　　Carbohydrate: 4 g　　Fat: 15 g　　Kilocalories: 250

Tandoori Sardine; South Indian Spiced Whitebait; Spicy Baked Trout

SPICY BAKED TROUT

4 fresh trout, about 250 g (10 oz) each
MARINADE:
2 tablespoons Mild Curry Paste (see page 8)
1 tablespoon plain or gram flour*
1 tablespoon natural yogurt
1 tablespoon sunflower oil
½ teaspoon chilli powder*
TO GARNISH:
lime slices, halved
dill sprigs

Mix the marinade ingredients together to make a paste. Coat the fish with the marinade and leave them to stand for 2–4 hours, no longer.

Bake in a preheated oven, 160°C, 325°F, Gas Mark 3 for 30 minutes.

Garnish with halved lime slices and sprigs of dill.

SERVES 4

Nutritional content per serving: Carbohydrate: 4 g   Fat: 18 g   Kilocalories: 420

DEVILLED SRI LANKAN SQUID

375 g (12 oz) squid
50 g (2 oz) plain flour
50 g (2 oz) semolina
2 eggs, beaten
vegetable oil for frying
lemon slices, quartered, to garnish
SPICES:
2 teaspoons Mild Curry Powder (see
    page 7)
1 teaspoon Garam Masala (see page 10)
1 teaspoon mango powder* (optional)

Clean the squid and remove the quill shaped back bone and ink sac. Slice it into rings. Combine the spices, flour and semolina on a flat plate. Dip the squid into the egg and coat with the flour mixture.

Heat the oil to 190°C, 375°F or until a cube of bread browns in 30 seconds. Carefully place the squid in the oil and deep-fry for 5–8 minutes, depending on thickness, until they are crisp and golden. Alternatively, shallow-fry in a frying-pan. Strain to remove excess oil. Garnish with lemon quarters and serve hot, with a salad.

SERVES 4 as a starter

Nutritional content per serving:	Carbohydrate: 22 g	Fat: 14 g	Fibre: 1 g	Kilocalories: 290

WHITE FISH IN COCONUT

4 tablespoons sunflower or mustard blend
    oil*
1 onion, chopped very finely
1 tablespoon Mild Curry Paste (see page 8)
flesh of ½ fresh coconut plus its milk or 2
    tablespoons desiccated coconut
300 ml (½ pint) milk
4 haddock or other white fish fillets, about
    175 g (6 oz) each
1 tablespoon chopped coriander*
salt
SPICES:
1 teaspoon black mustard seeds*
½ teaspoon turmeric*
TO GARNISH:
2 tablespoons shredded fresh coconut
coriander sprigs*

Heat the oil in a large flat frying pan and stir-fry the spices for 1 minute. Add the onion and continue to stir-fry for 3 minutes. Stir in the curry paste. Let the mixture simmer.

If using fresh coconut, purée the white flesh with the coconut milk in a food processor or blender. Alternatively mix the desiccated coconut with enough water to make a paste. Add the purée or paste to the frying pan and stir-fry to simmering point. Stir in the milk.

Place the fish fillets in the pan so that the sauce just covers them. Simmer gently for 10 minutes. Test the fish to see if it is cooked through. It should be almost ready, depending on thickness. Add the coriander and salt to taste. Continue to simmer for 2–3 minutes until the fish is completely cooked.

Transfer the fish and sauce carefully to a heated serving dish and serve immediately, garnished with coconut and coriander sprigs.

Microwave: Place the oil in a shallow cooking dish and cook on High Power for 2 minutes. Add the spices and cook on High Power for 2 minutes. Add the onion, cover and cook on High Power for 3 minutes. Stir in the curry paste and coconut mixture and cook on High Power for 2 minutes. Stir in the milk and add the fish, cover and cook on High Power for 6 minutes or until the fish is just cooked, stirring to rearrange the fish fillets once. Add the coriander and salt to taste. Cover and cook on High Power for 1–2 minutes, until hot and bubbly. Serve as above.

SERVES 4

Nutritional content per serving:	Carbohydrate: 6 g	Fat: 26 g	Fibre: 2 g	Kilocalories: 400

Devilled Sri Lankan Squid; White Fish in Coconut

SWEET AND SOUR PRAWNS

750 g (1½ lb) prawns, defrosted if frozen
3 tablespoons sunflower oil
300 ml (½ pint) Curry Purée (see page 9)
1 tablespoon Mild Curry Paste (see page 8)
1 tablespoon tomato purée
1 tablespoon prawn ballichow* (optional)
1 tablespoon brown sugar
2 tablespoons desiccated coconut
1 tablespoon tomato ketchup
1 tablespoon vinegar
1 tablespoon chopped coriander*
salt
SPICES:
1 teaspoon cumin seeds
1 teaspoon black mustard seeds*
1 teaspoon sesame seeds

Wash the prawns thoroughly, strain and set aside.

Heat the oil in a large frying pan or wok and stir-fry the spices for 1–2 minutes until they 'pop'. Add the curry purée and stir-fry for an additional 5 minutes. Add the curry paste, tomato purée, prawn ballichow, if using, sugar and coconut. Mix in water a little at a time to keep the sauce creamy.

When the sauce has reached simmering point add the prawns and more water if needed. Cook for 5 minutes and add the ketchup, vinegar, chopped coriander and salt to taste. Simmer for 5 more minutes. Do not overcook or the prawns will become rubbery. Serve immediately

SERVES 4

| Nutritional content per serving: | Carbohydrate: 11 g | Fat: 26 g | Fibre: 3 g | Kilocalories: 430 |

LOBSTER CURRY

2 whole cooked lobsters, about 750 g
   (1½ lb) each or 4 large cooked crayfish,
   defrosted if frozen
4 tablespoons sunflower oil
2 cloves garlic, chopped finely
1 onion, chopped finely
4 tomatoes, chopped finely
1 tablespoon chopped coriander*
2 teaspoons Garam Masala (see page 10)
SPICES:
1 teaspoon white cumin seeds
1 teaspoon black mustard seeds*
GOAN MARINADE:
2 tablespoons white wine vinegar plus juice
   of 2 lemons
2 tablespoons sunflower oil
2 teaspoons paprika
2 teaspoons ground coriander*
1 teaspoon ground cumin
1 teaspoon mustard powder
½–2 teaspoons chilli powder*
2 teaspoons brown sugar
½ teaspoon salt

Mix the marinade ingredients together to make a paste. Leave to stand and let the flavours blend while preparing the lobster. Halve the lobster shells with a cleaver or sharp knife and remove the meat from the shells and claws. Clean and retain the shells. Coat the meat thoroughly with the marinade and leave for 1–2 hours. Place the marinated lobster on a baking sheet and braise in a preheated oven 160°C, 325°, Gas Mark 3, for 10 minutes. Meanwhile, heat the oil in a large frying pan or wok. Stir-fry the spices for 1 minute. Add the garlic and stir-fry for 1 minute more. Add the onion and stir-fry for 3 minutes. Add the tomatoes, coriander and garam masala and bring to simmering point.

Remove the lobster from the oven and combine it with the sauce. Spoon it into the lobster shells, pouring the excess over each half. Serve at once.

SERVES 4

| Nutritional content per serving: | Carbohydrate: 8 g | Fat: 26 g | Fibre: 2 g | Kilocalories: 340 |

Lobster Curry; Sweet and Sour Prawns

MEAT DISHES

ALTHOUGH THE MAJORITY OF THE INDIAN POPULATION IS VEGETARIAN, THERE ARE OVER 200 MILLION MEAT EATERS IN THE CURRY LANDS. THE RECIPES IN THIS CHAPTER INCLUDE A GOOD SELECTION OF POPULAR FAVOURITES TOGETHER WITH SOME AUTHENTIC RECIPES THAT ARE LESS WELL KNOWN.

LAMB SHAHI KORMA

150 ml (5 fl oz) natural yogurt
750 g (1½ lb) lean lamb, diced
4 tablespoons concentrated butter or
  ghee*
300 ml (½ pint) Curry Purée (see page 9)
1 tablespoon Mild Curry Paste (see page 8)
1 tablespoon brown sugar
1 teaspoon salt
150 ml (5 fl oz) single cream
2 tablespoons chopped or ground almonds
2 teaspoons Garam Masala (see page 10)
1 tablespoon chopped coriander*
SPICES:
8 bay leaves
10 green cardamoms*
15 cm (6 inch) piece cinnamon stick
10 cloves
1 teaspoon fennel seeds*
1 teaspoon white cumin seeds
TO GARNISH:
flaked almonds, toasted
single cream
coriander leaves

Mix the yogurt with the lamb in a bowl. Cover and refrigerate for 24 hours. Heat the butter or ghee in a frying pan and fry the spices for 1 minute. Add the curry purée and stir-fry for 5 minutes. Stir in the curry paste, sugar and salt and bring to simmering point.

Transfer this mixture to a heavy 3 litre (5 pint) casserole and add the lamb and yogurt mixture. Combine the ingredients well. Place the lid on the casserole and bake in a preheated oven, 190°C, 375°F, Gas Mark 5, for 1 hour. After 20 minutes' cooking time add the cream, chopped almonds, garam masala and chopped coriander, with water if the mixture looks too dry. If at the end of cooking there is an excess of oil, spoon it off before serving. To serve, garnish with toasted almonds, a little cream and coriander leaves.

Microwave: Mix the yogurt with the lamb as above. Place the butter or ghee in a bowl and cook on High Power for 2 minutes to melt. Add the spices and cook on High Power for 2 minutes. Add the curry purée, curry paste, sugar and salt, stirring 3 times. Add the cream, almonds, garam masala and coriander, mixing well. Reduce the power to Medium, cover and cook for 20 minutes, stirring 3 times, or until tender. Serve as above.

SERVES 4

Nutritional content per serving:	Carbohydrate: 8 g	Fat: 35 g	Fibre: 2 g	Kilocalories: 600

LAMB BHOONA

THE BHOONA PROCESS IS A DRY-FRYING TECHNIQUE SO THIS CURRY, WHICH IS QUITE DARK IN APPEARANCE, SHOULD END UP FAIRLY DRY

4 tablespoons concentrated butter or
  ghee*
150 ml (¼ pint) Curry Purée (see page 9)
750 g (1½ lb) lean lamb, diced
1 tablespoon tomato purée
1 tablespoon desiccated coconut
2 teaspoons Garam Masala (page 10)
chilli powder to taste* (optional)
salt
parsley sprigs to garnish
SPICES:
4 bay leaves
6 small pieces cinnamon stick
6 cloves
1 teaspoon turmeric*

Heat the butter or ghee in a frying pan or wok. Fry the spices for 1 minute. Add the curry purée and stir-fry for 5 minutes. In a separate pan over a moderate heat fry the meat without oil for 10 minutes, so that it is sealed and brown on all sides. If any fat is released by the meat, strain it off. Add 1 tablespoon of cooked purée to the meat and stir-fry until it has been absorbed by the meat – about 2 minutes. Continue until all the purée is used up. The meat will look quite dry.

Transfer the meat to a heavy lidded casserole and bake in a preheated oven, 190°C, 375°F, Gas Mark 5, for 20 minutes. Add the tomato purée, coconut, garam masala, chilli powder, if using, and salt to taste. Replace in the oven and cook for a further 40 minutes. If at the end of cooking there is an excess of oil, spoon it off before serving. Garnish with parsley to serve.

SERVES 4

Nutritional content per serving:	Carbohydrate: 1 g	Fat: 33 g	Fibre: 1 g	Kilocalories: 525

Lamb Bhoona; Lamb Shahi Korma

RHOGAN GOSHT

750 g (1½ lb) lean lamb, diced
150 ml (5 fl oz) natural yogurt
4 tablespoons concentrated butter
2 cloves garlic, chopped finely
5 cm (2 inch) piece fresh root ginger, chopped finely
1 large onion, chopped finely
1 tablespoon Mild Curry Paste (see page 8)
1 × 425 g (14 oz) can tomatoes
1 red pepper, puréed
SPICES 1:
4 bay leaves
2 brown cardamoms*
4 green cardamoms*
15 cm (6 inch) piece cinnamon stick
6 cloves
1 teaspoon fennel seeds*
2 star anise*
SPICES 2:
1 tablespoon Garam Masala (see page 10)
2 teaspoons paprika

Mix the lamb, yogurt and first set of spices in a bowl. Cover and refrigerate for 24 hours. Heat the butter in a frying pan and stir-fry the garlic for 1 minute. Add the ginger and fry for 1 minute more. Add the onion and stir-fry for 5 more minutes. Add the paste, tomatoes, pepper and the meat mixture. Transfer to a casserole and bake in a preheated oven, 190°C, 375°F, Gas Mark 5, for 20 minutes. Add the second set of spices with a little water if necessary. Return to the oven and cook for 40 minutes. Serve with rice.

Microwave: Mix the lamb with the yogurt and spices as above. Place the butter in a bowl and cook on High Power for 2 minutes. Add the garlic and cook on High Power for 1 minute. Add the ginger and cook on High Power for 1 minute. Add the onion, cover and cook on High Power for 3 minutes. Add the curry paste, tomatoes and pepper, mixing well. Add the meat, cover and cook on High Power for 20 minutes, stirring 3 times. Add the second set of spices, blending well, return to the microwave, cover and cook on Medium Power for 20 minutes, stirring twice, until the lamb is tender.

SERVES 4

Nutritional content per serving:	Carbohydrate: 10 g	Fat: 31 g	Fibre: 2 g	Kilocalories: 550

Rhogan Gosht

Persian Khoresh

PERSIAN KHORESH

IT IS POSSIBLE CURRY ORIGINATED IN PERSIA; THIS AROMATIC 'KHORESH' COULD BE THE DISH FROM WHICH THE WORD 'CURRY' DERIVED

4 tablespoons concentrated butter or
  ghee*
I large onion, chopped finely
750 g (1 ½ lb) lean lamb, diced
I tablespoon lemon juice
2 tablespoons whole blanched almonds
I tablespoon pine kernels (optional)
I teaspoon dried barberry* (optional)
I teaspoon chopped mint or ½ teaspoon
  bottled mint
salt
brown sugar to taste
mint sprigs to garnish
SPICES:
2 teaspoons ground cinnamon or cassia
  bark*
I teaspoon turmeric*
I teaspoon ground white cumin
I teaspoon garlic powder
I teaspoon Garam Masala (see page 10)

Heat the butter or ghee in a frying pan. Stir-fry the spices for 1 minute; add the onion and continue to stir-fry for 5 minutes. Transfer the contents of the pan to a heavy lidded casserole. Stir in the meat and place the casserole in the centre of a preheated oven, 190°C, 375°F, Gas Mark 5, and bake for 20 minutes. Add the remaining ingredients, with a little water to moisten if necessary. Continue cooking for 40 minutes. Test the flavour: if it is too sour, add more sugar. If at the end of cooking there is an excess of oil, spoon it off. Garnish with mint.

Freezing: is recommended. When cold remove all the larger whole spices and store and freeze in an earthenware dish, foil or plastic container. This will keep for up to 3 months. Reheat in a covered dish in a preheated oven 180°C, 350°F, Gas Mark 4 for 45 minutes or cover and microwave on Defrost for 20–25 minutes, stirring once, then reheat on High Power for 8–10 minutes, stirring twice.

SERVES 4

Nutritional content per serving: Carbohydrate: 6 g   Fat: 37 g   Fibre: 2 g   Kilocalories: 583

LAMB WITH SPINACH

THE GREEN OF THE SPINACH IN THIS RECIPE KNOWN AS *SAG GOSHT*, GIVES IT AN INTERESTING APPEARANCE

500 g (1 lb) spinach
4 tablespoons concentrated butter or
  ghee*
300 ml (½ pint) Curry Purée (see page 9)
4 tomatoes, skinned and chopped
2 tablespoons Mild Curry Paste (see page
  8)
500 g (1 lb) lean lamb, diced
1 tablespoon Garam Masala (see page 10)
1 tablespoon dried fenugreek leaves*
salt

Prepare the spinach. If it is fresh, wash the leaves thoroughly and chop them roughly. If frozen, defrost it completely and drain well. If canned, strain off the excess liquid. Heat the butter or ghee in a large frying pan or wok. Stir-fry the curry purée for 5 minutes. Add the tomatoes, spinach and the curry paste. Simmer for 5 minutes, stirring occasionally, until the ingredients have blended. Add the lamb mixing it in well. Transfer the mixture to a heavy lidded casserole and bake in a preheated oven, 190°C, 375°F, Gas Mark 5 for 20 minutes. Add the garam masala, fenugreek and salt to taste, with a little water to moisten if necessary. Return to the oven and cook for a further 40 minutes. Spoon off any excess oil before serving.

SERVES 4

Nutritional content per serving:	Carbohydrate: 9 g	Fat: 31 g	Fibre: 1 g	Kilocalories: 480

LAMB DHANSAK

125 g (4 oz) red lentils
4 tablespoons concentrated butter or
  ghee*
300 ml (½ pint) Curry Purée (see page 9)
2 tablespoons Mild Curry Paste (see
  page 8)
1 × 425 g (14 oz) can ratatouille or home-
  made, cooked ratatouille or any
  combination of aubergine, tomato,
  spinach, pepper, courgette, potato, pea,
  bean and okra
500 g (1 lb) lean lamb, diced
1 tablespoon chopped coriander*
1 tablespoon brown sugar
1 tablespoon Garam Masala (see page 10)
salt
parsley sprigs to garnish

Sift through the lentils for grit. Soak them in twice their volume of water for 1–2 hours. Strain the lentils and cook them in an equal volume of boiling water for 30 minutes. Heat the butter or ghee in a frying pan. Stir-fry the curry purée for 5 minutes. Add the curry paste and stir in the ratatouille. Transfer this mixture to a heavy lidded casserole. Stir in the diced lamb and bake in a preheated oven, 190°C, 375°F, Gas Mark 5 for 20 minutes. Add the chopped coriander, sugar, garam masala, drained lentils and salt to taste with a little water to moisten if necessary. Return the casserole to the oven and cook for a further 40 minutes. If, at the end of the cooking time there is an excess of oil, spoon it off before serving. Garnish with parsley sprigs.

Microwave: Prepare the lentils and cook as above. Place the butter or ghee in a bowl and cook on High Power for 2 minutes. Add the curry purée and cook on High Power for 3 minutes, stirring once. Add the curry paste, ratatouille and lamb, mixing well. Cover and cook on High Power for 20 minutes, stirring 3 times. Add the coriander, sugar, garam masala, drained lentils and salt to taste. Reduce the power to Medium and cook for a further 20 minutes, stirring twice. Serve as above.

SERVES 4

Nutritional content per serving:	Carbohydrate: 28 g	Fat: 38 g	Fibre: 6 g	Kilocalories: 630

Lamb with Spinach; Lamb Dhansak

KASHMIRI LAMB

4 tablespoons concentrated butter or
   ghee*
300 ml (½ pint) Curry Purée (see page 9)
2 tablespoons Mild Curry Paste
   (see page 8)
625 g (1¼ lb) lean lamb, diced
125 g (4 oz) banana, pineapple and/or
 ·lychees, chopped
coriander sprigs to garnish

Heat the butter or ghee in a large frying pan or wok. Stir-fry the curry purée for 5 minutes. Add the curry paste and the lamb and continue to stir-fry until the meat is nicely brown all over. Transfer this mixture to a heavy lidded casserole with a little water (or juice from the canned fruit, if available). Place the casserole in a preheated oven, 190°C, 375°F, Gas Mark 5, for 1 hour. If at the end of the cooking time there is an excess of oil, spoon it off. Add the chopped fruit 5 minutes before serving. Serve hot, garnished with coriander.

Freezing: is recommended. When cold freeze in a dish. This will keep for up to 3 months. Reheat in a covered dish in a preheated oven 180°C, 350°F, Gas Mark 4 for 45 minutes or cover and microwave on Defrost for 20–25 minutes, stirring once, then reheat on High Power for 8–10 minutes, stirring twice.

SERVES 4

Nutritional content per serving:	Carbohydrate: 6 g	Fat: 32 g	Fibre: 2 g	Kilocalories: 500

LAMB WITH NUTS AND APRICOTS

75 ml (3 fl oz) vinegar
750 g (1½ lb) lean lamb, diced
4 tablespoons concentrated butter or
   ghee*
300 ml (½ pint) Curry Purée (see page 9)
6–8 dried apricots, sliced
3 tablespoons ground almonds
3 tablespoons mixed whole nuts, e.g.
   almonds, hazelnuts and pistachios
1 tablespoon brown sugar
1 tablespoon tomato ketchup
1 tablespoon Garam Masala (see page 10)
salt
rosemary sprigs to garnish
SPICES:
6 green cardamoms*
15 cm (6 inch) piece cinnamon stick or
   cassia bark*
12 cloves
2 teaspoons white cumin seeds

Mix the vinegar with the spices to make a runny paste. Combine the paste and the lamb and place into a lidded casserole and bake in a preheated oven, 190°C, 375°F, Gas Mark 5 for 20 minutes.

Meanwhile, heat the butter or ghee in a large frying pan or wok. Stir-fry the curry purée for 5 minutes. Add the dried apricots, mixing well. Add this mixture to the casserole, with the ground almonds, whole nuts, sugar, ketchup, garam masala and salt to taste. Stir in a little water to moisten if necessary. Return the casserole to the oven and continue to cook for a further 40 minutes. If there then is an excess of oil, spoon it off. Garnish with rosemary.

Microwave: Prepare the lamb as above and place in a casserole. Cover and cook on High Power for 20 minutes, stirring twice. Place the butter or ghee in a bowl and cook on High Power for 2 minutes. Add the purée and cook on High Power for 3 minutes, stirring once. Add the apricots and mix into the meat mixture with the almonds, nuts, sugar, ketchup, garam masala and salt. Reduce the power to Medium and cook for 25 minutes or until tender, stirring 3 times.

SERVES 4

Nutritional content per serving:	Carbohydrate: 16 g	Fat: 44 g	Fibre: 8 g	Kilocalories: 705

Kashmiri Lamb; Lamb with Nuts and Apricots

LAMB TIKKA

500 g (1 lb) lean lamb, diced
175 g (6 oz) (⅔ quantity) Tandoori
  Marinade (see page 26)
TO GARNISH:
carrot flowers
parsley sprigs

Combine the lamb and marinade in a bowl. Cover and leave in the refrigerator for about 24 hours.

If using a barbecue, thread the tikkas loosely on to metal skewers and place them over the coals for 15–20 minutes, turning frequently. If using the grill, place the tikkas on the wire tray and cook under a medium heat for 15–20 minutes, turning them once half-way through the cooking time. To bake, place the tikkas on a baking sheet and coat with any extra marinade. Bake in a preheated oven, 180°C, 350°F, Gas Mark 4 for 30 minutes, turning them over after 20 minutes. Serve hot, garnished with carrot flowers and parsley.

Freezing: is recommended. When cold store and freeze in a polythene bag, foil or plastic container. This will keep for up to 3 months. Reheat in a preheated oven 180°C, 350°F, Gas Mark 4 for 30 minutes or cover and microwave on Defrost for 10–15 minutes, then reheat on High Power for 5 minutes or until hot.

SERVES 4 as a starter

Nutritional content per serving: Carbohydrate: 2 g   Fat: 11 g   Kilocalories: 206

LAMB TIKKA MASALA

750 g (1½ lb) lean lamb, diced
275 g (9 oz) (1 quantity) Tandoori
  Marinade (see page 26)
SAUCE:
4 tablespoons concentrated butter or
  ghee*
300 ml (½ pint) Curry Purée (see page 9)
1 tablespoon Tandoori Paste (see page 10)
2 teaspoons tomato purée
2 tomatoes, skinned and chopped
1 red pepper, puréed
1 tablespoon chopped coriander*
1 tablespoon ground almonds
2 tablespoons single cream
white sugar
salt
TO GARNISH:
lime slices, quartered
parsley sprigs

Cook the tikkas as above reserving 2 tablespoons of the marinade. While they are cooking make the sauce.

Heat the butter or ghee in a large frying pan or wok. Stir-fry the curry purée for 5 minutes. Add the tandoori paste and the reserved marinade and stir-fry for 2 minutes. Add the tomato purée, tomatoes and red pepper. Bring to simmering point and add a little water, if necessary, to achieve a creamy textured sauce. Add the coriander, almonds, cream and sugar and salt to taste. When the tikkas are cooked, stir them into the sauce. If you have baked them and there is any marinade left, add it to the sauce. Garnish with lime slices and parsley.

Freezing: is recommended. When cold store and freeze in a foil or plastic container. This will keep for up to 3 months. Reheat in a preheated oven 180°C, 350°F, Gas Mark 4 for 30 minutes or cover and microwave on Defrost for 20–25 minutes, stirring once, then reheat on High Power for 8–10 minutes, stirring twice.

SERVES 4

Nutritional content per serving: Carbohydrate: 4 g   Fat: 35 g   Fibre: 2 g   Kilocalories: 565

Lamb Tikka; Lamb Tikka Masala

MUGHLAI BEEF

750 g (1½ lb) lean stewing steak, cubed

4 tablespoons concentrated butter or
  ghee*

2 cloves garlic, chopped finely

5 cm (2 inch) piece fresh root ginger,
  chopped finely

1 large onion, sliced thinly

1 tablespoon Mild Curry Paste (see page 8)

50 g (2 oz) unsalted cashew nuts, chopped

2 tablespoons ground almonds

75 ml (3 fl oz) single cream

1 tablespoon chopped coriander*

MARINADE PASTE:

75 ml (3 fl oz) natural yogurt

2 teaspoons Mild Curry Powder (see page 7)

2 teaspoons white sugar

½ teaspoon Aromatic Salt (see page 8)

TO GARNISH:

1 tablespoon unsalted cashew nuts,
  chopped

coriander leaves*

Mix the stewing steak and the marinade paste ingredients in a bowl. Cover and put in the refrigerator for up to 24 hours. Heat the butter or ghee in a large frying pan or wok. Stir-fry the garlic for 1 minute; add the ginger and stir-fry for 1 minute more; add the onion and stir-fry for a further 5 minutes. Add the curry paste and a little water – enough to loosen the mixture without making it too runny. Add the cashews and ground almonds.

Transfer the mixture to a heavy lidded casserole and stir in the steak and marinade. Place in a preheated oven, 190°C, 375°F, Gas Mark 5, and bake for 20 minutes. Add the cream and chopped coriander and continue cooking for 30 minutes. If at the end of cooking there is an excess of oil, spoon it off. Garnish with chopped cashew nuts and coriander.

SERVES 4

Nutritional content per serving: Carbohydrate: 14 g   Fat: 42 g   Fibre: 2 g   Kilocalories: 600

Mughlai Beef

Beef Pasanda

BEEF PASANDA

750 g (1 ½ lb) lean beef rump, fillet or
   topside
150 ml (¼ pint) red wine
4 tablespoons vegetable oil
300 ml (½ pint) Curry Purée (see page 9)
1 tablespoon Mild Curry Paste (see page 8)
175 ml (6 fl oz) milk
2 tablespoons ground almonds
2 tablespoons desiccated coconut
4 tablespoons double cream
salt
SPICES:
2 teaspoons Garam Masala (see page 10)
1 teaspoon ground mace
½ teaspoon ground cinnamon
TO GARNISH:
parsley sprigs
chopped pistachio nuts

Slice the beef into 4 steaks. Beat with the back of a wooden spoon until they are 5 mm (¼ inch) thick. Cut each steak in half to give 8 pieces. Marinate the steaks in the wine and spices for up to 24 hours. Heat the oil in a frying pan or wok and stir-fry the curry purée for 5 minutes. Add the curry paste and mix well. Lift the steaks out of the marinade and add to the pan 2 at a time. Fry the steaks quickly to seal – allow about 20 seconds on each side. When all the steaks are in the pan and are brown, add the remaining ingredients, including the marinade. Simmer for 10 minutes, until the meat is cooked. Transfer to a heated dish and pour on the cream. Serve with rice and garnish with parsley and pistachio nuts.

Freezing: is recommended. When cold remove any larger whole spices and store and freeze in an earthenware dish, foil or plastic container. This will keep for up to 3 months. Reheat in a covered dish in a preheated oven 180°C, 350°F, Gas Mark 4 for 45 minutes or cover and microwave on Defrost for 20–25 minutes, stirring once, then reheat on High Power for 8–10 minutes, stirring twice.

SERVES 4

Nutritional content per serving: Carbohydrate: 7 g   Fat: 50 g   Fibre: 3 g   Kilocalories: 740

METHI GOSHT

CUBES OF BEEF COOKED WITH DRIED FENUGREEK* (METHI) LEAF PRODUCES A MOST SAVOURY CURRY

4 tablespoons concentrated butter or
    ghee*
300 ml (½ pint) Curry Purée (see page 9)
2 tablespoons Mild Curry Paste (see page
    8)
750 g (1 ½ lb) stewing beef, diced
4 tomatoes, chopped
4 tablespoons dried fenugreek leaves*
1 tablespoon Garam Masala (see page 10)
salt
2 tablespoons chopped parsley to garnish

Heat the butter or ghee in a large frying pan or wok and stir-fry the curry purée for 5 minutes. Stir the curry paste in well to blend and add the diced beef. Stir-fry for about 5 minutes more to seal the meat.

Transfer the meat and sauce to a heavy lidded casserole and bake in a preheated oven, 190°C, 375°F, Gas Mark 5 for 20 minutes. Stir in the tomatoes, fenugreek, garam masala and salt to taste, with a little water to moisten if necessary. Continue cooking for a further 25 minutes. If at the end of cooking there is an excess of oil, spoon it off before serving. Garnish with chopped parsley.

Freezing: is recommended. When cold remove any larger whole spices and store and freeze in an earthenware dish, foil or plastic container. This will keep for up to 3 months. Reheat in a covered dish in a preheated oven 180°C, 350°F, Gas Mark 4 for 45 minutes or cover and microwave on Defrost for 20–25 minutes, stirring once, then reheat on High Power for 8–10 minutes, stirring twice.

SERVES 4

Nutritional content per serving:	Carbohydrate: 5 g	Fat: 31 g	Fibre: 2 g	Kilocalories: 475

ACHAR GOSHT

THIS NEPALESE RECIPE USES A PICKLE BASE WITH CUBED BEEF AND SLICES OF MANGO ADDED TOWARDS THE END OF THE COOKING

4 tablespoons concentrated butter or
    ghee*
300 ml (½ pint) Curry Purée (see page 9)
1 tablespoon Mild Curry Paste (see page 8)
750 g (1 ½ lb) stewing beef, diced
1 fresh mango
3 tablespoons mild mango or brinjal*
    pickle, chopped finely
1 tablespoon chopped coriander*
salt
TO GARNISH:
fresh mango slices
parsley sprigs

Heat the butter or ghee in a large frying pan or wok and stir-fry the curry purée for 5 minutes. Stir in the curry paste and the meat, combining the ingredients well. Continue frying until the meat is sealed, about 5 minutes.

Transfer to a heavy lidded casserole and place in a preheated oven 190°C, 375°F, Gas Mark 5 for 20 minutes.

Meanwhile scoop all the flesh from the mango and work it to a purée. Add it to the casserole with the chopped pickle, coriander and salt to taste, with a little water to moisten if necessary.

Return the casserole to the oven for a further 25 minutes. Spoon off any excess oil at the end of the cooking time, before serving. Garnish with fresh mango slices and parsley sprigs.

SERVES 4

Nutritional content per serving:	Carbohydrate: 10 g	Fat: 32 g	Fibre: 2 g	Kilocalories: 490

Methi Gosht; Achar Gosht

KEEMA

THIS RELATIVELY INEXPENSIVE, TASTY AND EASILY MADE MINCED MEAT CURRY IS SADLY UNDERRATED

4 tablespoons concentrated butter or
  ghee*
300 ml (½ pint) Curry Purée (see page 9)
2 tablespoons Mild Curry Paste (see page 8)
750 g (1½ lb) minced beef
4 tomatoes, skinned and chopped
½ red pepper, chopped finely
½ green pepper, chopped finely
2 teaspoons Garam Masala (see page 10)
2 teaspoons poppy seeds
1–3 teaspoons chilli powder* (optional)
1 tablespoon desiccated coconut or
  coconut powder*
salt
parsley sprigs to garnish

Heat the butter or ghee in a large frying pan or wok and stir-fry the curry purée for 5 minutes. Add the curry paste and the beef and stir-fry for about 10 minutes more. Add the tomatoes and peppers. Transfer everything to a heavy lidded casserole and bake in a preheated oven, 190°C, 375°F, Gas Mark 5, for 20 minutes. Add the remaining ingredients and return to the oven for a further 25 minutes. Spoon off any excess oil before serving. Garnish with parsley sprigs.

Freezing: is recommended. When cold store and freeze in an earthenware dish, foil or plastic container. This will keep for up to 3 months. Reheat in a covered dish in a preheated oven 180°C, 350°F, Gas Mark 4 for 45 minutes or cover and microwave on Defrost for 5–10 minutes, then reheat on Medium for 3–5 minutes.

SERVES 4

Nutritional content per serving:	Carbohydrate: 7 g	Fat: 59 g	Fibre: 2 g	Kilocalories: 705

Keema

Kofta

KOFTA

750 g (1½ lb) minced beef
2–4 cloves garlic, chopped
5cm (2inch) piece fresh root ginger, chopped
2 tablespoons chopped coriander*
1 tablespoon dried mint
4 tablespoons vegetable oil or ghee*
300 ml (½ pint) Curry Purée (see page 9)
1 tablespoon Mild Curry Paste (see page 8)
150 ml (5.2 oz) carton natural yogurt
150 ml (5.2 oz) carton single cream
20 strands saffron* (optional)
salt
basil sprigs to garnish
GROUND SPICES:
1 teaspoon ground coriander*
1 teaspoon ground cumin
½ teaspoon chilli powder* (optional)
1 teaspoon paprika
1 teaspoon mango powder* (optional)
WHOLE SPICES:
1 teaspoon white cumin seeds
1 teaspoon black mustard seeds*
1 teaspoon sesame seeds
½ teaspoon wild onion seeds* (optional)

Put the minced beef, garlic, ginger, coriander, mint and ground spices into a food processor and work to obtain a finely ground texture. Alternatively, mince the minced beef, herbs and spices twice in a hand mincer. Mould the mixture into small balls, no larger than 3 cm (1¼ inches) in diameter. Place the balls on a baking sheet and bake in a preheated oven, 160°C, 325°F, Mark 3 for 15 minutes.

While the balls are cooking make the sauce. Heat the oil or ghee in a large frying pan or wok. Stir-fry the whole spices for 1 minute. Add the curry purée and stir-fry for 5 minutes more. Stir in the curry paste and remove the pan from the heat for 5 minutes. When the mixture has cooled slightly, add the yogurt and cream. Replace the pan over the heat and let the mixture come to simmering point – do not let it boil. Take the balls from the oven and add them and any juice to the pan. Add the saffron, if using, and season with salt to taste. Garnish with basil, and serve immediately with rice.

Microwave: Prepare the beef balls as above. Place on a plate and cook on High Power for 8–9 minutes, turning once. To make the sauce, place the oil or ghee in a dish and cook on High Power for 2 minutes. Add the spices and cook on High Power for 2 minutes, stirring once. Add the curry purée and cook on High Power for 3 minutes, stirring once. Stir in the curry paste and cook on High Power for 1 minute. Cool slightly before adding the yogurt and cream, stirring well. Add the beef balls and saffron if using. Season to taste and serve.

SERVES 4

Nutritional content per serving: Carbohydrate: 10 g   Fat: 63 g   Fibre: 1 g   Kilocalories: 760

CHINESE PORK CURRY

2 tablespoons cornflour
6 tablespoons milk
4 tablespoons vegetable oil
1 onion, puréed
750 g (1½ lb) pork fillet, chopped
1 teaspoon orange squash
1 tablespoon tomato purée
1 tablespoon white sugar
salt
2 blood orange slices, quartered
parsley sprigs to garnish
SPICES:
1 tablespoon Mild Curry Paste (see page 8)
1 teaspoon garlic powder
2 teaspoons Chinese five spice powder*
1–2 teaspoons chilli powder* (optional)

Mix the cornflour and milk to a smooth paste and set aside. Mix the spices with enough water to make a thickish paste. Heat the oil in a large frying pan or wok. Stir-fry the spice paste for 5 minutes. Add the puréed onion and continue stir-frying for 5 minutes. Stir in the cornflour paste and continue to stir as the sauce thickens, adding water as you go.

Transfer the sauce with the pork to a heavy lidded casserole and bake in a preheated oven, 190°C, 375°F, Gas Mark 5, for 20 minutes. Add the remaining ingredients, with a little water to moisten if necessary, and season with salt to taste. Return to the oven and continue to cook for 40 minutes more. Serve hot, with orange slices and garnished with parsley sprigs.

SERVES 4

Nutritional content per serving:	Carbohydrate: 12 g	Fat: 29 g	Fibre: 1 g	Kilocalories: 540

THAI PORK RED CURRY

4 tablespoons concentrated butter or
   ghee*
2–8 cloves garlic, chopped finely
1 onion, sliced
1 tablespoon Mild Curry Paste (see page 8)
300 ml (½ pint) water
2.5 cm (1 inch) piece fresh root ginger,
   sliced thinly
1–6 fresh red chillies*, sliced
2 tablespoons puréed anchovies
750 g (1½ lb) pork fillet, diced
1 red pepper, puréed
6–8 dried or fresh lime leaves* (optional)
2 tablespoons desiccated coconut mixed
   with water
1 tablespoon chopped coriander leaves*
2 teaspoons chopped basil leaves
salt
TO GARNISH:
1 tablespoon chopped coriander leaves*
coarsely grated fresh coconut
75 g (3 oz) small pink shrimps
basil sprigs

Heat the butter or ghee in a large frying pan or wok and stir-fry the garlic for 1 minute. Add the onion and stir-fry until it is soft and transparent. Add the curry paste. Blend in and add the water – Thai curries are fairly runny. Add the ginger, chillies, and the anchovies, and simmer for 3–4 minutes. Transfer this mixture to a heavy lidded casserole and stir in the pork. Place in a preheated oven, 190°C, 375°F, Gas Mark 5 and bake for 20 minutes. Add the remaining ingredients, with a little water to moisten if necessary, and replace in the oven to cook for 40 minutes more. Just before serving, season with salt to taste and spoon off any excess oil. Garnish with chopped coriander, coconut, shrimps and basil. Serve at once.

SERVES 4

Nutritional content per serving:	Carbohydrate: 5 g	Fat: 34 g	Fibre: 3 g	Kilocalories: 560

Chinese Pork Curry; Thai Pork Red Curry

Veal Mooli

VEAL MOOLI

FROM THE SOUTH OF INDIA COMES THE SUBTLE MOOLI RECIPE, WHICH SUITS FISH, CHICKEN AND VEGETABLES AS WELL AS VEAL

250 ml (8 fl oz) milk
4 tablespoons sunflower oil
2–4 large cloves garlic, chopped finely
1 large onion, chopped finely
750 g (1 ½ lb) veal escalope, diced
milk of 1 coconut and flesh of ½ a coconut
   or 2 tablespoons desiccated coconut and
   125 ml (4 fl oz) milk or water
1–6 fresh green chillies*, sliced
20 strands saffron* (optional)
2 tablespoons lemon juice
salt
coarsely grated coconut to garnish
SPICES:
¼ teaspoon asafoetida* (optional)
½ teaspoon ground ginger
½ teaspoon mango powder* (optional)
½ teaspoon turmeric*
1 teaspoon sesame seeds
1 teaspoon black mustard seeds*
1 teaspoon white cumin seeds

Combine the spices with the milk to make a thin paste. Let it stand for about 30 minutes. Heat the oil in a large frying pan or wok and stir-fry the garlic for 1 minute. Add the onion and stir-fry for 3 or 4 minutes more. Blend in the spice paste. When it has reached simmering point, add the veal. Continue to simmer, stirring occasionally, for 10 minutes. Add the coconut mixture and 1–6 chillies, depending on how hot a flavour you like. The consistency of the sauce should be fairly thin. Continue to simmer for 10 minutes or until the meat is tender. Add the saffron, if using, and lemon juice and season with salt to taste. Serve immediately, garnished with grated coconut.

Freezing: is recommended. When cold store and freeze in an earthenware dish, foil or plastic container. This will keep for up to 3 months. Reheat in a covered dish in a preheated oven 180°C, 350°F, Gas Mark 4 for 45 minutes or cover and microwave on Defrost for 20–25 minutes, stirring once, then reheat on High Power for 8–10 minutes, stirring twice.

SERVES 4

Nutritional content per serving: Carbohydrate: 8 g   Fat: 29 g   Fibre: 2 g   Kilocalories: 470

VEAL PASANDA

8 veal escalopes, about 75 g (3 oz) each
4 tablespoons lemon juice
4 tablespoons concentrated butter or
  ghee*
300 ml (½ pint) Curry Purée (see page 9)
75 ml (3 fl oz) natural yogurt
75 ml (3 fl oz) single cream
1 tablespoon brown sugar
1 tablespoon ground almonds
1 tablespoon desiccated coconut
20 strands saffron* (optional)
salt
watercress sprigs to garnish
WHOLE SPICES:
2 teaspoons poppy seeds
1 teaspoon sesame seeds
1 teaspoon white cumin seeds
½ teaspoon black cumin seeds
GROUND SPICES:
2 teaspoons ground coriander*
1 teaspoon ground cumin
½ teaspoon turmeric*

Beat the escalopes until they are about 5 mm (¼ inch) thick. Steep them in the lemon juice until required.

Heat the butter or ghee in a large frying pan or wok. Stir-fry the whole spices for 1 minute; add the curry purée and stir-fry for 5 minutes more. Add the ground spices and stir-fry for 3 or 4 minutes. Finally add the veal and lemon juice. Stir-fry for 10 minutes, turning the pieces from time to time so that they cook evenly.

Add the yogurt, cream, sugar, ground almonds, coconut and saffron if using. Season with salt to taste and continue to simmer for 10 more minutes, until the veal is perfectly tender. It may need a little longer. To serve, garnish with sprigs of watercress.

Freezing: is recommended. When cold freeze in a plastic container. This will keep for up to 3 months. Reheat in a dish in a preheated oven 180°, 350°, Gas Mark 4 for 45 minutes or cover and microwave on Defrost for 20–25 minutes, stirring once, then reheat on High Power for 8–10 minutes, stirring twice.

SERVES 4

Nutritional content per serving: Carbohydrate: 11 g   Fat: 32 g   Fibre: 2 g   Kilocalories: 470

Veal Pasanda

THE MAHARAJAH'S ROYAL VENISON CURRY

750 g (1 1/2 lb) venison, diced
300 ml (1/2 pint) red wine
4 tablespoons vegetable oil
300 ml (1/2 pint) Curry Purée (see page 9)
2 tablespoons Mild Curry Paste (see page 8)
1 × 425 g (14 oz) can tomatoes, strained
1 red pepper, chopped finely
1 tablespoon Garam Masala (see page 10)
2 tablespoons dried fenugreek leaves*
salt
SPICES (roast and ground):
1 teaspoon fennel seeds*
8 green cardamoms*
1 teaspoon fenugreek seeds*
1 teaspoon black mustard seeds*
2 teaspoons white cumin seeds

Wash the meat in two or three changes of cold water, drain and pat dry with kitchen paper. Place it in a 3 litre (5 pint) casserole with the wine and the spices. Cover and marinate for 6–24 hours.

Heat the oil in a large frying pan or wok. Stir-fry the curry purée for 5 minutes. Blend in the curry paste. Add this mixture to the venison in the casserole. Place in a preheated oven, 190°C, 375°F, Gas Mark 5 and bake for 20 minutes. Add the tomatoes, pepper, garam masala and fenugreek, with a little water or juice from the canned tomatoes, to moisten, if necessary. Replace the casserole in the oven and continue to cook for 55 minutes. Check half-way through the cooking time to ensure that the meat is not becoming dry; if it is add a little more water or tomato juice. Serve hot.

SERVES 4

Nutritional content per serving:	Carbohydrate: 10 g	Fat: 34 g	Fibre: 2 g	Kilocalories: 690

BURMESE PORK AND BEAN SPROUT CURRY

625 g (1 1/4 lb) pork fillet, diced
4 tablespoons concentrated butter or
  ghee*
300 ml (1/2 pint) Curry Purée (see page 9)
1 tablespoon Mild Curry Paste (see page 8)
4 tablespoons fish sauce* or puréed
  anchovies
1–6 fresh green chillies*, chopped
1 tablespoon mild mango or brinjal* pickle,
  chopped
1 tablespoon vinegar
125 g (4 oz) bean sprouts
flesh of 1/2 fresh coconut plus milk of 1
  coconut or 2 tablespoons desiccated
  coconut
1 tablespoon tomato purée
2 teaspoons Garam Masala (see page 10)

Place the pork in a 3 litre (5 pint) lidded casserole. Heat the butter or ghee in a large frying pan or wok. Stir-fry the curry purée for 5 minutes. Add the curry paste, fish sauce or puréed anchovies, chillies to taste, mango or brinjal pickle and vinegar. Continue to stir-fry for 1–2 minutes to blend. Add this to the pork.

Place the casserole in a preheated oven, 190°C, 375°F, Gas Mark 5, and bake for 1 hour. After 20 minutes check to see if the pork is getting too dry, and add a little water if necessary.

Wash the bean sprouts in several changes of water. Blanch them and add them with the remaining ingredients after 40 minutes, cooking time. Before serving, spoon off excess oil. Serve hot.

Microwave: Place the pork in a dish. Place the butter or ghee in a bowl and cook on High Power for 2 minutes. Add the purée and cook on High Power for 3 minutes, stirring once. Add the paste, fish sauce or anchovies, chillies, mango or brinjal pickle and vinegar and cook on High Power for 2 minutes. Add the sauce to the pork, mixing well. Cover and cook on High Power for 20 minutes, stirring 3 times. Add the blanched bean sprouts and remaining ingredients, reduce the power to Medium and cook for 20 minutes, stirring twice. Serve hot.

SERVES 4

Nutritional content per serving:	Carbohydrate: 11 g	Fat: 34 g	Fibre: 2 g	Kilocalories: 550

The Maharajah's Royal Venison Curry; Burmese Pork and Bean Sprout Curry

CHILLI FRY

THIS IS A FAIRLY DRY DISH WITH A SPICY GINGERY FLAVOUR

4 tablespoons vegetable oil
750 g (1 ½ lb) lean sirloin steak, diced
2–8 cloves garlic, chopped finely
7 cm (3 inch) piece fresh root ginger,
   chopped finely
1 teaspoon turmeric*
2 teaspoons paprika
1 × 425 g (14 oz) can tomatoes
1 large onion, puréed
2–6 fresh green chillies*, chopped
2–4 teaspoons chilli powder*
salt
SPICES (roast and ground):
2 teaspoons coriander seeds*
1 teaspoon white cumin seeds
½ teaspoon fennel seeds*
½ teaspoon fenugreek seeds*

Heat the oil in a large frying pan or wok. Add the diced steak a little at a time, stir-frying until it is all sealed – about 5 minutes. Add the garlic, according to taste and stir-fry for about 2 minutes, until it has blended with the meat; add the ginger and stir-fry for 2 minutes more. Sprinkle in the roast and ground spices, the turmeric and paprika and stir-fry until the pieces of meat are coated with garlic, ginger and spices. The meat should be dry without sticking to the pan. Strain the tomatoes and use the juice to moisten the meat if necessary.

Add the puréed onion a tablespoon at a time, allowing each spoonful to be absorbed by the meat before adding the next. Stir-fry for another 3–4 minutes. By now the meat should have cooked for about 20 minutes and will be half cooked. Add the remaining tomato juice, the tomatoes, chillies and chilli powder to taste (remembering that this dish is meant to be hot). Season with salt to taste, cover and continue to cook for 20 minutes, or until the beef is quite tender. Serve hot.

SERVES 4

| Nutritional content per serving: | Carbohydrate: 12 g | Fat: 60 g | Fibre: 2 g | Kilocalories: 720 |

Chilli Fry

Madras Meat

MADRAS MEAT

4 tablespoons concentrated butter or
  ghee*

300 ml (½ pint) Curry Purée (see page 9)

2 tablespoons Mild Curry Paste (see page 8)

750 g (1½ lb) lean stewing steak or lamb,
  cut into cubes

6 canned or fresh tomatoes, skinned and
  chopped

2–6 fresh green or red chillies*, chopped

1 red pepper, chopped

1 tablespoon ground almonds

1 tablespoon Garam Masala (see page 10)

1 tablespoon dried fenugreek leaves*

4 tablespoons lemon juice

SPICES:

½ teaspoon turmeric*

½ teaspoon ground cumin

1–3 teaspoons pepper

1–3 teaspoons chilli powder*

Heat the butter or ghee in a large frying pan or wok. Sprinkle over
the spices and stir briskly for 20 seconds. Add the purée and stir-fry
for 5 minutes. Blend in the paste and bring to simmering point.

Transfer to a heavy lidded casserole with the diced meat and
bake in a preheated oven, 190°C, 375°F, Gas Mark 5 for 20 minutes.
Strain the tomatoes if they are canned and reserve the liquid. Add
the tomatoes and all the remaining ingredients to the casserole, with
a little water or tomato juice to moisten if necessary.

Return to the oven and cook for 25 minutes for beef or 40
minutes for lamb. If at the end there is an excess of oil, spoon it off.

Freezing: is recommended. When cold store and freeze in an
earthenware dish, foil or plastic container. This will keep for up to
3 months. Reheat in a covered dish in a preheated oven 180°C,
350°F, Gas Mark 4 for 45 minutes or cover and microwave on
Defrost for 20–25 minutes, stirring once, then reheat on High Power
for 8–10 minutes, stirring twice.

SERVES 4

Nutritional content per serving: Carbohydrate: 8 g   Fat: 70 g   Fibre: 2 g   Kilocalories: 800

BANGALORE PHALL

THIS RECIPE IS A PURE INVENTION OF WESTERN RESTAURANTS. THE PRIMARY SPICE USED IS CHILLI POWDER* AND IT IS VERY HOT INDEED. THOSE WHO RELISH THE HEAT SHOULD BE ENCOURAGED TO ACCOMPANY IT WITH CHILLI PICKLE

4 tablespoons concentrated butter or ghee*
300 ml (½ pint) Curry Purée (see page 9)
2 tablespoons Mild Curry Paste (see page 8)
750 g (1½ lb) lean lamb or stewing steak, cut into cubes
2–6 fresh green or red chillies*, chopped finely
salt
parsley sprigs to garnish
SPICES:
2 teaspoons paprika
2–6 teaspoons pepper
2–8 teaspoons chilli powder*

Heat the butter or ghee in a large frying pan or wok and stir-fry the curry purée for 5 minutes. Add the curry paste and the spices, mixing them in well, and stir-fry for 5 more minutes. Transfer to a heavy lidded casserole with the diced meat, and place in a preheated oven, 190°C, 375°F, Gas Mark 5, for 20 minutes. Add chillies to taste, season with salt, and add a little water if necessary to moisten. Return the casserole to the oven and continue cooking for 25 minutes for beef, 40 minutes for lamb. If at the end of the cooking time there is an excess of oil, spoon it off before serving. Garnish with parsley sprigs.

Microwave: Place the butter or ghee in a bowl and cook on High Power for 2 minutes. Add the curry purée and cook on High Power for 3 minutes, stirring once. Add the curry paste and the spices and cook on High Power for 3 minutes, stirring once. Add the lamb or steak (good quality beef is essential), cover and cook on High Power for 20 minutes, stirring 3 times. Add chillies and salt to taste. Reduce the power level to Medium and cook for a further 15–20 minutes, until the meat is tender, stirring twice. Serve as above.

SERVES 4

Nutritional content per serving:	Carbohydrate: 4 g	Fat: 40 g	Fibre: 1 g	Kilocalories: 600

GOAN VINDALOO

750 g (1½ lb) pork fillet or tenderloin, diced
200 ml (7 fl oz) vinegar
2–6 teaspoons chilli powder*
4 tablespoons concentrated butter or ghee*
300 ml (½ pint) Curry Purée (see page 9)
4–8 fresh or dried red chillies*
salt
basil sprigs to garnish
SPICES (roast and ground):
2 teaspoons coriander seeds*
1 teaspoon white cumin seeds
10 cm (4 inch) piece cinnamon stick
12 cloves
12 green cardamoms*
2 teaspoons black peppercorns

Place the pork in a china or glass dish with the vinegar and chilli powder to taste. Cover and refrigerate for 24 hours.

Mix the spices with enough water to make a paste. Heat the butter or ghee in a large frying pan or wok and stir-fry the curry purée for 5 minutes. Add the spice paste, stir-frying for 2 minutes more. Lift the pieces of pork out of the marinade, reserving the liquid, and combine them with the ingredients in the pan. Transfer this mixture to a heavy lidded casserole and bake in a preheated oven, 190°C, 375°F, Gas Mark 5 for 1 hour, adding chillies to taste after 20 minutes cooking time, with a little salt, and marinade to moisten if necessary. If at the end of the cooking time there is an excess of oil, spoon it off before serving. Garnish with basil sprigs.

SERVES 4

Nutritional content per serving:	Carbohydrate: 6 g	Fat: 19 g	Fibre: 1 g	Kilocalories: 420

Bangalore Phall; Goan Vindaloo

POULTRY AND GAME

ALTHOUGH IT IS SAID THAT WILD CHICKEN ORIGINATED IN THE JUNGLES OF INDIA, LIKE MOST POULTRY AND GAME IT IS CONSIDERED TO BE A LUXURY IN THE SUB-CONTINENT. IN BRITAIN, HOWEVER, WE ARE LUCKY THAT CHICKEN IS INEXPENSIVE, PLENTIFUL AND LIKE GAME, IDEALLY SUITED TO CURRY TECHNIQUES.

CHICKEN KORMA

4 tablespoons concentrated butter
750 g (1½ lb) skinless chicken breast
300 ml (½ pint) Curry Purée (see page 9)
50 ml (2 fl oz) natural yogurt
142 ml (5 fl oz) carton single cream
1 tablespoon ground almonds
1 tablespoon chopped hazelnuts
1 tablespoon chopped pistachio nuts
2 teaspoons Garam Masala (see page 10)
20 strands saffron* (optional)
salt
parsley sprigs to garnish
SPICES:
1 teaspoon white cumin seeds
15 cm (6 inch) cinnamon stick
10 cloves
4 brown cardamoms*
1 teaspoon poppy seeds
1 teaspoon sesame seeds
½ teaspoon wild onion seeds* (optional)
½ teaspoon turmeric*

Heat the butter in a large frying pan or wok and stir-fry the spices for 1 minute. Cut the chicken into cubes and add to the frying pan or wok. Continue to stir-fry until they go white – about 3–4 minutes. Add the curry purée, yogurt and cream, mixing well. Bring the mixture to simmering point, stirring from time to time.

After 10 minutes add all the nuts, the garam masala and saffron, if using. Add a little water if necessary. Simmer for 5 minutes more and season with salt to taste. Transfer to a heated serving dish and garnish with parsley sprigs.

Freezing: is recommended. When cold remove any larger whole spices and store in an earthenware dish, foil or plastic container. This will keep for up to 3 months. Reheat in a covered dish in a preheated oven 180°C, 350°F, Gas Mark 4 for 45 minutes or cover and microwave on Defrost for 20–25 minutes, stirring once, then reheat on High Power for 8–10 minutes, stirring twice.

SERVES 4

Nutritional content per serving: Carbohydrate: 4 g   Fat: 30 g   Fibre: 1 g   Kilocalories: 495

Chicken Korma

CHICKEN JALFREZI

6 tablespoons concentrated butter or
  ghee*
2–6 cloves garlic, chopped finely
5 cm (2 inch) piece fresh root ginger, sliced
  finely
1 large onion, sliced thinly
750 g (1½ lb) boneless, skinless chicken
  breast, diced
1 tablespoon Mild Curry Paste (see page 8)
½ red pepper, chopped
½ green pepper, chopped
2 tomatoes, skinned and chopped
1 tablespoon chopped coriander leaves*
SPICES:
1 teaspoon white cumin seeds
1 teaspoon black mustard seeds*

Heat the butter or ghee in a large frying pan or wok. Stir-fry the spices for 1 minute. Add the garlic and stir-fry for 1 minute more. Add the ginger and stir-fry for 2 minutes. Add the sliced onion and stir-fry until golden – about 5 minutes.

Combine the chicken pieces with the ingredients in the pan stirring and turning for 5 more minutes. Add all the remaining ingredients and 1 or 2 tablespoons of water and stir-fry for around 10 more minutes. Serve immediately.

Variation

Chilli Chicken: This is a much hotter version of the above. Prepare as above but add 2–10 chopped green chillies instead of the peppers. (The quantity of chillies depends on your heat threshold.)

Freezing: is recommended. When cold store and freeze in an earthenware dish, foil or plastic container. This will keep for up to 3 months. Reheat in a covered dish in a preheated oven 180°C, 350°F, Gas Mark 4 for 45 minutes or cover and microwave on Defrost for 20–25 minutes, stirring once, then reheat on High Power for 8–10 minutes, stirring twice.

SERVES 4

Nutritional content per serving:	Carbohydrate: 7 g	Fat: 32 g	Fibre: 2 g	Kilocalories: 525

COCONUT CHICKEN

6 tablespoons sunflower oil
750 g (1½ lb) boneless, skinless chicken
  breast, diced
2–6 cloves garlic, chopped finely
300 ml (½ pint) milk
50 ml (2 fl oz) natural yogurt
2 tablespoons desiccated coconut
1 tablespoon chopped coriander*
salt
SPICES:
1 teaspoon black mustard seeds*
1 teaspoon sesame seeds
1 teaspoon poppy seeds
½ teaspoon black cumin seeds
TO GARNISH:
20 unsalted cashew nuts, fried until golden
coriander sprigs

Heat the oil in a frying pan or wok and stir-fry the spices for 1 minute. Add the chicken and stir-fry for about 5 minutes, turning frequently, until they are white all over. Add the garlic, milk, yogurt and coconut. Simmer for 5 minutes, stirring from time to time. Add the coriander and simmer for 5–10 minutes, until the chicken is tender. Season to taste. Transfer to a heated dish. Garnish with fried cashews and coriander.

Freezing: is recommended. When cold, freeze in an plastic container. This will keep for up to 3 months. Reheat in a covered dish in a preheated oven 180°C, 350°F, Gas Mark 4 for 45 minutes or cover and microwave on Defrost for 20–25 minutes, stirring once, then reheat on High Power for 8–10 minutes, stirring twice.

SERVES 4

Nutritional content per serving:	Carbohydrate: 9 g	Fat: 41 g	Fibre: 2 g	Kilocalories: 620

Chicken Jalfrezi; Coconut Chicken

CHICKEN TIKKA MASALA

750 g (1½ lb) chicken tikka cooked as in
  recipe below
9–12 tablespoons fresh lemon juice or 6
  tablespoons bottled lemon juice
275 ml (9 fl oz) (1 quantity) Tandoori
  Marinade (see page 26)
SAUCE:
4 tablespoons concentrated butter or ghee*
300 ml (½ pint) Curry Purée (see page 9)
1 tablespoon Tandoori Paste (see page 10)
2 tablespoons Tandoori Marinade
2 teaspoons tomato purée
2 tomatoes, skinned and chopped
1 red pepper, puréed
1 tablespoon chopped coriander*
1 tablespoon ground almonds
2 tablespoons single cream
white sugar
salt
TO GARNISH:
lemon slices, halved
coriander sprigs

Cook the tikkas exactly as described in the following recipe.

Whilst they are cooking, make the sauce. Heat the butter or ghee in a large frying pan or wok. Stir-fry the curry purée for 5 minutes. Add the tandoori paste and marinade and stir-fry for 2 minutes. Add the tomato purée, tomatoes and pepper. Bring to simmering point and add a little water, if necessary to achieve a creamy textured sauce. Add the coriander, almonds, cream and sugar and salt to taste. When the tikkas are cooked, stir them into the sauce. Garnish with lemon slices and coriander sprigs.

Microwave: Prepare the chicken tikka as described in Chicken Tikka Tandoori. To make the sauce, place the butter or ghee in a bowl and cook on High Power for 2 minutes. Add the curry purée and cook on High Power for 3 minutes, stirring once. Add the tandoori paste and marinade and cook on High Power for 1 minute, stirring once. Add the tomato purée, tomatoes and pepper and cook on High Power for 1 minute. Add the coriander, almonds, cream and sugar and salt to taste and cook on High Power for ½ minute. Stir the cooked chicken tikkas into the sauce to serve. Garnish as above.

SERVES 4

Nutritional content per serving: Carbohydrate: 6 g   Fat: 33 g   Fibre: 1 g   Kilocalories: 550

CHICKEN TIKKA TANDOORI

TRADITIONALLY THIS POPULAR DISH IS COOKED IN A TANDOOR (A BEEHIVE-SHAPED CLAY OVEN). THE CHICKEN PIECES (TIKKAS) ARE PLACED ON LONG SKEWERS AND BAKED OVER CHARCOAL FOR 10–15 MINUTES

500 g (1 lb) boneless, skinless chicken
  breast, diced
6–8 tablespoons fresh lemon juice or
  4 tablespoons bottled lemon juice
275 ml (9 fl oz) (1 quantity) Tandoori
  Marinade (see page 26)

Place the chicken in a large bowl and add the lemon juice, working it in with the fingers, to 'de-grease' the chicken in preparation for the marinade. Leave to stand for 1 hour.

Strain off and discard the juices, then combine the tandoori marinade with the chicken. Cover and refrigerate for a minimum of 6 hours, or overnight, but preferably for 24 hours.

Thread the tikkas on to metal skewers and place over the barbecue coals for 10–15 minutes, turning them 2 or 3 times. Alternatively, the tikkas can be grilled, baked in a preheated oven, 190°C, 375°F, Gas Mark 5, or even stir-fried (without oil) for about 15 minutes in each case. Serve with a salad.

SERVES 4 as a starter

Nutritional content per serving: Carbohydrate: 2 g   Fat: 6 g   Kilocalories: 205

Chicken Tikka Masala; Chicken Tikka Tandoori

Butter Chicken

BUTTER CHICKEN

750 g (1 ½ lb) chicken breast, diced
7 tablespoons vinegar
1 tablespoon chopped mixed herbs to
   garnish
MARINADE:
2–6 cloves garlic
5 cm (2 inch) piece fresh root ginger
2 tablespoons Mild Curry Paste (see page 8)
1 tablespoon chopped coriander*
1–4 fresh green chillies* (optional)
1 teaspoon dried mint
142 ml (5.2 fl oz) carton natural yogurt
½ teaspoon salt
SAUCE:
6 tablespoons concentrated butter
1 teaspoon white cumin seeds
1 teaspoon black cumin seeds
1 small onion, sliced thinly
7 tablespoons single cream
1 tablespoon Garam Masala (see page 10)

Combine the marinade ingredients in a blender or food processor, and set aside for the flavours to infuse. Put the chicken into a bowl and add the vinegar, mixing well, and set aside for 1–2 hours. Spoon the marinade into the bowl with the chicken and vinegar and mix well. Cover and refrigerate overnight or for up to 24 hours.

Transfer the chicken pieces and all the marinade to a roasting tin. Place in a preheated oven, 160°C, 325°F, Gas Mark 3 and bake for 20 minutes. Meanwhile, make the sauce. Heat the butter in a large frying pan or wok and stir-fry the cumin for 1 minutes. Add the onion and stir-fry until it is crisp and golden. Add the cream and garam masala and simmer gently.

As soon as the chicken is cooked, transfer it to the sauce in the frying pan or wok and mix well. Transfer to a heated serving dish and serve at once, sprinkled with mixed herbs.

SERVES 4

Nutritional content per serving: Carbohydrate: 6 g   Fat: 40 g   Fibre: 1 g   Kilocalories: 590

CHICKEN KOFTA

750 g (1 ½ lb) boneless, skinless chicken
  breast, diced
3.5 cm (1 ½ inch) piece fresh root ginger,
  chopped
3–6 cloves garlic, chopped
1 tablespoon chopped coriander*
SPICES:
3 teaspoons Tandoori Masala (see page 10)
1 ½ teaspoons Garam Masala (see page 10)
1 ½ teaspoons garlic powder
1 ½ teaspoons Mild Curry Powder (see
  page 7)
SAUCE:
2 tablespoons concentrated butter or
  ghee*
300 ml (½ pint) Curry Purée (see page 9)
1 tablespoon Mild Curry Paste (see page 8)
7 tablespoons single cream
50 g (2 oz) desiccated coconut or creamed
  coconut block*, chopped finely
150 ml (¼ pint) dry white wine (optional)
1 tablespoon chopped coriander*
salt
TO GARNISH:
1 tablespoon chopped flaked almonds,
  toasted
watercress sprigs

Mix the spices together. Place the chicken, ginger, garlic and coriander in a food processor and work to a fine-ground texture. Process in 3 or 4 batches for ease of working. Transfer the minced chicken to a mixing bowl and work in the spices thoroughly with your fingers. Divide into 16 equal portions and roll them into balls. You can make 24 smaller balls if you prefer. Place the balls on a baking sheet and bake in a preheated oven, 160°C, 325°F, Gas Mark 3 for 15 minutes, or 12 minutes for the smaller balls.

Meanwhile, make the sauce. Heat the butter or ghee in a large frying pan or wok and stir-fry the curry purée for 5 minutes. Add the curry paste, cream and coconut and continue to stir until the coconut melts, if using creamed coconut. Gently add the cooked kofta with the wine, if using, and chopped coriander. Simmer for no more than 5 minutes. Transfer to a heated serving dish, sprinkle with almonds, garnish with sprigs of watercress and serve immediately.

Microwave: Prepare the chicken balls as above and place on a large plate or microwave roasting trivet and cook on High Power for 6–8 minutes or until just cooked, turning over once. To make the sauce, place the butter or ghee in a bowl and cook on High Power for 2 minutes. Add the curry purée and cook on High for 3 minutes, stirring once. Add the coconut and cook on High Power for 1 minute, stirring once. Add the kofta with the wine, if using and chopped coriander. Cover and cook on High Power for 3 minutes, stirring once. Serve as above.

SERVES 4

Nutritional content per serving: Carbohydrate: 6 g   Fat: 31 g   Fibre: 3 g   Kilocalories: 505

MURGHI MASALA

4 boneless, skinless chicken breasts each
  weighing about 150 g (5 oz)
175 g (6 oz) uncooked Chicken Kofta or
  Shami Kebab mixture (see pages 64 or 65)
parsley sprigs to garnish
COATING SAUCE:
75 ml (3 fl oz) natural yogurt
2 tablespoons Mild Curry Powder or Paste
  (see pages 7 or 8)
1 teaspoon Garam Masala (see page 10)
1 teaspoon Tandoori Masala (see page 10)
1 teaspoon Aromatic Salt (see page 8)

Carefully slit each breast to make a pocket, and stuff it with the kebab mixture of your choice. Do not overfill the pocket. If there is any mixture left, shape it into rissoles and cook with the breasts.

Place the stuffed breasts on to a baking sheet. Mix the ingredients for the coating sauce together and spread it thickly over the chicken. Place the baking sheet in a preheated oven, 160°C, 325°F, Gas Mark 3 and bake for 20 minutes. Transfer the breasts to a heated dish and garnish with parsley. Serve the breasts with Kofta Sauce (see above) if you prefer a more moist dish.

SERVES 4

Nutritional content per serving: Carbohydrate: 3 g   Fat: 9 g   Kilocalories: 300

Chicken Shami Kebab; Chicken Kofta; Murghi Masala

CHICKEN SHAMI KEBAB

500 g (1 lb) boneless, skinless chicken
  breast, diced
2.5cm (1 inch) piece fresh root ginger,
  chopped
2–4 cloves garlic, chopped
1 tablespoon chopped coriander*
SPICES:
2 teaspoons Tandoori Masala (see page 10)
1 teaspoon Garam Masala (see page 10)
1 teaspoon garlic powder
1 teaspoon Mild Curry Powder (see page 7)
TO GARNISH:
lime wedges
cress

Mix the spices together. Place the chicken, ginger, garlic and
coriander in a food processor and work to give a fine-ground
texture. Process in 3 or 4 batches. Transfer to a mixing bowl and
work the spices in thoroughly with your fingers. Divide the mixture
into 4 equal portions and shape them into sausages. Make the
'sausages' around metal skewers if cooking on a barbecue or grill.
This is not essential if you are baking them in the oven. Cook over
charcoal, or under the grill on a moderate heat for 10–15 minutes,
turning the skewers from time to time. Alternatively, bake in a
preheated oven, 160°C, 325°F, Gas Mark 3 for the same time.
Garnish with lime wedges and cress and serve with Mint Raita (see
page 94).

SERVES 4 as starter

Nutritional content per serving: Carbohydrate: 3 g   Fat: 6 g   Kilocalories: 200

SRI LANKAN DUCK

4 duck breasts, each weighing about 250 g
(8 oz)
3 tablespoons concentrated butter or
ghee*
300 ml (½ pint) Curry Purée (see page 9)
3½ oz (100 g) desiccated coconut or
creamed coconut block*
1 teaspoon vinegar
1 tablespoon brown sugar
salt
parsley sprigs to garnish
WHOLE SPICES:
1 teaspoon white cumin seeds
1 teaspoon panch phoran* (optional)
SPICES (roast and ground):
2 teaspoons coriander seeds*
1 teaspoon ground cinnamon
1 teaspoon white cumin seed
1 teaspoon fennel seeds*
8 green cardamoms*
6 cloves

Using a sharp knife, remove the skin and fat from the duck and cut the flesh into cubes. Add a little water to the roast and ground spices to make a paste. Heat the butter or ghee in a frying pan and stir-fry the whole spices for 1 minute. Add the curry purée and stir-fry for 5 minutes. Add the spice paste and stir-fry for 2–3 minutes more.

Combine this mixture with the duck in a casserole and bake in a preheated oven, 190°C, 375°F, Gas Mark 5 for 45 minutes, adding the coconut, vinegar, sugar and salt to taste after 20 minutes. Before serving, spoon off any excess oil and garnish with parsley.

Microwave: Prepare the duck and spice paste as above. Place the butter or ghee in a bowl and cook on High Power for 2 minutes. Add the whole spices and cook on High Power for 2 minutes. Add the curry purée and cook on High Power for 3 minutes, stirring once. Add the spice paste and cook on High Power for 1 minute. Add the duck and mix. Cover and cook on High Power for 15 minutes, stirring once. Add the coconut, vinegar, sugar and salt, reduce the power to Medium and cook for 15 minutes, stirring once, until tender.

SERVES 4

Nutritional content per serving: Carbohydrate: 10 g   Fat: 34 g   Fibre: 6 g   Kilocalories: 550

DUCK PASANDA

PASANDA MEANS 'BEATEN MEAT'. IN THIS RECIPE PIECES OF SKINNED DUCK BREAST ARE BEATEN, MARINATED OVERNIGHT IN RED WINE THEN SIMMERED IN CURRY SAUCE TO PRODUCE A DISH OF DISTINCTION

4 duck breasts, each weighing about 250 g
    (8 oz)
125 ml (4 fl oz) red wine
3 tablespoons concentrated butter or
    ghee*
300 ml (½ pint) Curry Purée (see page 9)
1 tablespoon Mild Curry Paste (see page 8)
1½ teaspoons Tandoori Masala (see
    page 10)
200 ml (7 fl oz) milk (approximately)
2 teaspoons Garam Masala (see page 10)
2 tablespoons desiccated coconut or
    coconut powder*
75 ml (3 fl oz) single cream
1 tablespoon chopped coriander*
salt

Carefully remove the skin and fat from the duck breasts with a sharp knife. Halve each breast along the long side to give 8 pieces. Place the pieces between sheets of greaseproof paper and beat them flat, increasing their original size by half and making them about 5 mm (¼ inch) thick. Place the pieces in a shallow dish and cover them with the red wine. Leave to marinate for at least 2 hours, overnight, or for a maximum of 24 hours.

To make the sauce, heat the butter or ghee in a frying pan or wok and stir-fry the curry purée for 5 minutes; add the paste and tandoori masala and stir-fry for a further 3–4 minutes. As soon as these ingredients have blended, add about half the milk with the wine from the marinade in order to make a fairly liquid consistency. Bring the sauce up to simmering point and place the duck pasandas in the pan, making sure they are covered with the sauce. Reduce the heat and let the duck simmer gently for 20 minutes, stirring from time to time to ensure it is not sticking. Do not cook the duck too quickly or the pieces will toughen and lose their shape.

Add the garam masala, coconut, cream and coriander and mix them in well. Continue to simmer for 10 minutes or so, adding the remaining milk a little at a time as required. Keeping the liquid balance correct is extremely important: by gradually reducing the sauce you should finally achieve a thickish creamy consistency but while the duck is still cooking the sauce must be relatively liquid. Season with salt to taste and transfer to a heated dish to serve.

Freezing: is recommended. When cold store and freeze in an earthenware dish, foil or plastic container. This will keep for up to 3 months. Reheat in a covered dish in a preheated oven 180°C, 350°F, Gas Mark 4 for 45 minutes or cover and microwave on Defrost for 20–25 minutes, stirring once, then reheat on High Power for 8–10 minutes, stirring twice.

SERVES 4

Nutritional content per serving:	Carbohydrate: 7 g	Fat: 30 g	Fibre: 2 g	Kilocalories: 525

Duck Pasanda; Sri Lankan Duck

TURKEY MALAYA

THIS RECIPE IS IDEALLY SUITED TO TURKEY, AND CONTAINS TYPICAL MALAYAN INGREDIENTS

4 tablespoons concentrated butter or
 ghee*
300 ml (½ pint) Curry Purée (see page 9)
2 tablespoons Mild Curry Paste (see page 8)
750 g (1½ lb) skinless turkey breast or leg
 meat, diced
I red pepper, chopped
100 g (3½ oz) desiccated coconut or
 creamed coconut block*
125 ml (4 fl oz) milk
I tablespoon fish sauce (nam pla)* or
 puréed anchovies
SPICES:
2 teaspoons Garam Masala (see page 10)
I teaspoon five-spice powder
½ teaspoon lemon grass powder (optional)
TO GARNISH:
unsalted peanuts, fried and chopped
pineapple, fresh or canned, chopped
dill sprigs

Heat the butter or ghee in a large frying pan or wok and stir-fry the curry purée for 5 minutes. Add the curry paste and mix it in well.

Transfer this mixture to a heavy lidded casserole with the turkey pieces and place in a preheated oven, 190°C, 375°F, Gas Mark 5 for 20 minutes. Add the spices, chopped red pepper, coconut, milk and fish sauce, and return to the oven to cook for 25 minutes more. If at the end of the cooking time there is an excess of oil, spoon it off before serving. Transfer to a heated dish and garnish with the peanuts, pineapple pieces, dill sprigs and serve with prawn crackers.

Microwave: Place the butter or ghee in a bowl and cook on High Power for 2 minutes. Add the curry purée and cook on High Power for 3 minutes, stirring once. Add the curry paste and turkey and cook on High Power for 10 minutes, stirring once. Add the spices, red pepper, coconut, milk and fish sauce or puréed anchovies, mixing well. Cover and cook on High Power for 10 minutes, stirring once. Serve as above.

SERVES 4

Nutritional content per serving:	Carbohydrate: 7 g	Fat: 47 g	Kilocalories: 630

TURKEY DO-PIAZA

'DO' MEANS TWO, 'PIAZA' MEANS ONION, WHICH MEANS THIS DISH CONTAINS TWICE AS MUCH ONION AS ANY OTHER RECIPE. THE ONION GIVES A SWEETISH TASTE THAT SUITS TURKEY VERY WELL

6 tablespoons concentrated butter or
 ghee*
I large onion, sliced thinly
300 ml (½ pint) Curry Purée (see page 9)
2 tablespoons Mild Curry Paste (see page 8)
750 g (1½ lb) skinless turkey breast or leg
 meat, diced
I tablespoon tomato ketchup
I teaspoon tomato purée
I tablespoon brown sugar
2 teaspoons Garam Masala (see page 10)
salt
watercress sprigs to garnish

Heat the butter or ghee in a large frying pan or wok, stir-fry the sliced onion for 5 minutes or until soft and transparent. Add the curry purée and continue frying for 5 more minutes. Stir in the curry paste and bring the mixture to simmering point.

Transfer the mixture to a heavy lidded casserole and add the diced turkey. Place the casserole in a preheated oven, 190°C, 375°F, Gas Mark 5 and cook for 20 minutes.

Add the tomato ketchup, tomato purée, sugar and garam masala, with a little water to moisten if necessary. Season with salt and return the casserole to the oven for a further 25 minutes. If at the end of cooking there is an excess of oil, spoon it off before serving. Garnish with watercress.

SERVES 4

Nutritional content per serving:	Carbohydrate: 12 g	Fat: 37 g	Fibre: I g	Kilocalories: 550

Turkey Malaya; Turkey Do-Piaza

BAKED SPICY QUAIL

4 whole quails

watercress sprigs to garnish

MARINADE:

142 ml (5.2 fl oz) carton natural yogurt

2 cloves garlic, chopped finely

75 g (3 oz) finely chopped onion

2 tablespoons Mild Curry Paste (see page 8)

2 teaspoons Garam Masala (see page 10)

½ teaspoon salt

BASTING LIQUID:

125 ml (4 fl oz) white wine

125 ml (4 fl oz) double cream

2 teaspoons brown sugar

1 tablespoon Mild Curry Paste (see page 8)

Combine the marinade ingredients in a large bowl and set aside for the flavours to blend. Wash the quails, taking care to rinse the inside cavity well with a clean tea towel or kitchen paper. Place the quail in a deep dish and coat them liberally with the marinade. Cover the dish and leave to stand in the refrigerator for up to 24 hours.

Place the quails in a roasting tin and bake in a preheated oven, 160°C, 325°F, Gas Mark 3 for 15 minutes. Prepare the basting liquid: in a small saucepan heat the wine to boiling point. Reduce the heat and stir in the cream, sugar and curry paste. Continue to stir for 2–3 minutes to dissolve the sugar and blend the mixture. After 10 minutes' cooking time, pour the hot basting liquid over the quails and return them to the oven for 5 minutes. To serve, place the quails on individual dishes and pour over the basting liquid. Garnish with sprigs of watercress.

SERVES 4

Nutritional content per serving: Carbohydrate: 11 g   Fat: 29 g   Kilocalories: 445

Baked Spicy Quail

The Maharajah's Stuffed Quail

THE MAHARAJAH'S STUFFED QUAIL

4 whole quails
125 g (4 oz) Basmati or long-grain rice,
   cooked and allowed to cool
MARINADE:
275 ml (9 fl oz) (1 quantity) Tandoori
   Marinade (see page 26)
GLAZE:
4 tablespoons clear honey
1 tablespoon Worcestershire sauce

If you have the time and the patience the quails can be boned. To do this use a small paring knife and small sharp scissors. Cut open the underside of each quail from front to back and flatten it out to a rectangular shape. Carefully remove the rib cage and leg bones, keeping the skin and flesh intact. Leave the wing bones in place.

Wash and dry the quails then make the marinade in a large bowl. Place the quails in the marinade, then leave to stand in the refrigerator for up to 24 hours.

To make the stuffing, mix a little marinade with the rice to make it easy to mould. For each bird, take 1 tablespoon of rice and round it into a shape the size of a ping-pong ball. Place into the cavity of each quail. Alternatively if you have boned the quail fold the quail around the rice ball, tucking in the skin and meat to give a firm quail that has assumed its original shape. Place the stuffed quails, breast side up in a roasting tin. Place in a preheated oven 160°C, 37.5°F, Gas Mark 3 for 15 minutes. After 10 minutes, heat the honey and Worcestershire sauce to make the glaze and pour it over the quails. Bake for 5 minutes, garnish with parsley and serve with rice and a salad.

SERVES 4

Nutritional content per serving: Carbohydrate: 40 g   Fat: 6 g   Fibre: 2 g   Kilocalories: 355

JAIPURI PARTRIDGE OR PHEASANT

4 small partridge, total weight about 1.5 kg (3 lb) or 2 small pheasants of same total weight
450 ml (¾ pint) game stock or water
4 carrots, shredded
6 shallots or pickling onions
4 tablespoons sunflower or mustard blend oil*
2 cloves garlic, chopped finely
5 cm (2 inch) piece fresh root ginger, chopped
1 onion, chopped
1 tablespoon Mild Curry Paste (see page 8)
2 tablespoons ground almonds
2 tablespoons desiccated coconut
dill sprigs to garnish
SPICES:
6 green cardamoms*
6 cloves
10 cm (4 inch) piece cinnamon stick or cassia bark*
1 teaspoon white cumin seeds
½ teaspoon fennel seeds*
½ teaspoon fenugreek seeds*
4 bay leaves
½ teaspoon Aromatic Salt (see page 8)
SCRAMBLED EGG:
25 g (1 oz) butter
3 eggs
1 teaspoon garlic powder
1 teaspoon Mild Curry Powder (see page 7)
1 tablespoon hazelnuts
1 tablespoon pistachio nuts
½ teaspoon Aromatic Salt

Skin the birds and wipe them inside and out with a clean damp cloth. Cut them into quarters with a cleaver and/or a heavy sharp knife.

Bring the stock or water to the boil in a 3.5 litre (5 pint) saucepan with the spices. Place the carrots, shallots or pickling onions and pieces of meat into the pan. Simmer for 20 minutes, so that the meat is half cooked and the water slightly reduced. Strain off the liquid and reserve. Leave the meat aside until it is cool enough to handle.

Meanwhile heat the oil in a large frying pan or wok and stir-fry the garlic for 1 minute. Add the ginger and stir-fry for 2 minutes more. Add the onion and stir-fry for another 5 minutes. Stir in the curry paste and the reserved liquid and bring the mixture to simmering point. Remove the flesh of the partridge or pheasant from the bones (leaving the leg meat on the bone if preferred). Place the meat and the contents of the frying pan or wok into the saucepan. Bring back to simmering point and continue to cook for about 20 more minutes, so that the liquid reduces further. It should be fairly dry, but not sticking to the pan. Stir in the almonds and coconut and increase the heat briefly so that the meat is heated through. The consistency should be fairly dry, but not sticking to the pan.

Transfer to a heated dish and keep hot while preparing the eggs. Melt the butter in a pan. Beat the eggs in a bowl with the garlic and curry powder, nuts and salt. Pour this into the pan and cook over a moderate heat, stirring. When the eggs are cooked but soft, spoon them over the meat. Garnish with dill and serve at once.

Microwave: Prepare and simmer the birds as above and cook with the vegetables conventionally until half-cooked. Place the oil in a large heatproof bowl and cook on High Power for 2 minutes. Add the garlic and cook on High Power for 1 minute. Add the ginger and cook on High Power for 1 minute. Add the onion and cook on High Power for 3 minutes, stirring once. Stir in the curry paste and three-quarters of the reserved liquid (discard the remainder) and cook on High Power for 2–3 minutes or until simmering. Remove the meat from the bones and add to the bowl. Cook on High Power for 8–10 minutes, until the meat is cooked and the mixture is fairly thick, stirring twice. Add the ground almonds and coconut and cook on High Power for 3 minutes, stirring once. Keep hot while preparing the eggs. Prepare the egg mixture as above. Place in a bowl with the butter and cook on High Power for 2¼–2½ minutes, stirring 3 times, until cooked but soft. Stand for 2 minutes before serving.

SERVES 4

Nutritional content per serving: Carbohydrate: 12 g   Fat: 52 g   Fibre: 6 g   Kilocalories: 890

Jaipuri Partridge

VEGETABLE DISHES

THERE ARE MORE THAN 700 MILLION VEGETARIANS IN INDIA, MORE THAN IN ANY OTHER COUNTRY. THEREFORE IT IS NOT SURPRISING THAT INDIAN COOKERY ABOUNDS IN IDEAS FOR PREPARING VEGETABLES WITH IMAGINATION. THESE RECIPES CAN MAKE MAIN DISHES OR CAN BE USED TO ACCOMPANY OTHER DISHES.

BOMBAY POTATO

THIS TASTY DISH USES POTATOES IN A MEDIUM-HOT CURRY SAUCE. SMALL NEW POTATOES ARE PERFECT FOR THIS RECIPE

4 tablespoons vegetable oil
150 ml (¼ pint) Curry Purée (see page 9)
1 tablespoon Mild Curry Paste (see page 8)
2 tomatoes, sliced thinly
750 g (1½ lb) cooked potatoes
Aromatic Salt (see page 8)
1 tablespoon chopped mixed herbs to
  garnish

Heat the oil in a large frying pan or wok and stir-fry the curry purée for 2–3 minutes. Add the curry paste and bring the mixture to simmering point. Add the tomatoes.

When the sauce is simmering again, add the potatoes and stir gently until they are heated through. Season with aromatic salt to taste, sprinkle with the herbs and serve at once.

SERVES 4

Nutritional content per serving:	Carbohydrate: 38 g	Fat: 17 g	Fibre: 2 g	Kilocalories: 300

MALAI KOFTA

THE BALLS (KOFTAS) FOR THIS CURRY ARE MADE FROM GRATED COURGETTE MIXED WITH POTATO AND PLAIN OR GRAM FLOUR, AND AFTER DEEP-FRYING THEY ARE IMMERSED IN A LIGHT CREAMY SAUCE (MALAI)

KOFTAS:
2 tablespoons plain or gram flour*
500 g (1 lb) mashed potatoes
4 courgettes, shredded
1–4 green chillies*, chopped
1 tablespoon chopped coriander*
semolina to coat the kofta
oil for deep-frying
SPICES:
1 tablespoon Mild Curry Powder (see page 7)
½ teaspoon garlic powder
1 teaspoon Garam Masala (see page 10)
SAUCE:
4 tablespoons sunflower oil
300 ml (½ pint) Curry Purée (see page 9)
1 tablespoon Mild Curry Paste (see page 8)
175 ml (6 fl oz) milk
125 ml (4 fl oz) single cream
1 tablespoon desiccated coconut
1 tablespoon ground almonds
125 ml (4 fl oz) white wine
salt
TO GARNISH:
1 tablespoon coarsely chopped pistachio nuts
dill sprigs

In a bowl combine the flour, mashed potato, courgettes, chillies, coriander and spices to make a smooth mixture. Divide the mixture into 4, then shape 6 balls from each portion, making a total of 24 balls. Heat the oil to 190°C, 375°F or until a cube of bread browns in 30 seconds. Roll each ball in semolina. Deep-fry the koftas 8 at a time for 5 minutes or until golden all over. Lift out of the oil with a slotted spoon. Keep them warm while preparing the sauce.

Heat the sunflower oil in a large frying pan or wok and stir-fry the curry purée for 5 minutes. Add the curry paste and blend it in well. Add the milk and cream, the coconut, ground almonds and wine. Season with salt to taste. Still stirring, bring the sauce to simmering point. If you want a thinner sauce add a little water. Fold in the koftas and cook briefly to heat them through. Transfer to a heated dish, garnish with pistachio nuts and sprigs of dill and serve immediately.

Freezing: is recommended for the kofta before cooking. Place the uncooked kofta in a single layer on a tray and open-freeze. When frozen, store and freeze in a polythene bag. These will keep for up to 3 months. These can be fried from frozen, there is no need to defrost them.

SERVES 4

Nutritional content per serving:	Carbohydrate: 40 g	Fat: 20 g	Fibre: 4 g	Kilocalories: 370

Malai Kofta; Bombay Potato

SPICED ROAST POTATOES MAKHANWALLA

4 large potatoes, peeled
275 ml (9 fl oz) (1 quantity) Tandoori
  Marinade (see page 26)
4 tablespoons vegetable oil
TO GARNISH:
Aromatic Salt (see page 8)
Garam Masala (see page 10)
parsley sprigs

Boil the whole potatoes for 10 minutes. Strain and leave to cool. When cool enough to handle, prick with a fork and score all over to help the marinade to hold. Place in a large bowl and coat with the marinade. Cover and refrigerate for 12–24 hours.

Place the potatoes and all the marinade in a roasting tin. Bake in a preheated oven 160°C, 325°F, Gas Mark 3 for 15 minutes. Prick the potatoes with a skewer to check that they are cooked – if ready it will go in without resistance. To finish, baste the potatoes with oil and return to the oven for 5 to 10 more minutes. Serve hot, sprinkled with aromatic salt, and garam masala and garnished with parsley.

SERVES 4

Nutritional content per serving:	Carbohydrate: 40 g	Fat: 16 g	Fibre: 2 g	Kilocalories: 320

POTATO SALLIS

1.5 kg (3 lb) potatoes (about 8–10)
vegetable oil for deep-frying
2 tablespoons Garam Masala (see page 10)
2 teaspoons Aromatic Salt (see page 8)
½–2 teaspoons chilli powder* (optional)

Slice 2 potatoes at a time into very thin chips, using a chip-cutter or a knife – do not prepare more than 2 at a time, or they will discolour. Deep-fry immediately for 8–10 minutes in oil heated to 190°C, 375°F or until a cube of bread browns in 30 seconds. Lift the sallis out of the oil, strain and place on kitchen paper to remove excess oil. Repeat the process until all the potatoes have been used. Sprinkle the sallis with garam masala, aromatic salt and chilli to taste, if using. Serve hot at once or allow to become completely cool and store.

SERVES 10 as a snack

Nutritional content per serving:	Carbohydrate: 75 g	Fat: 1 g	Fibre: 4 g	Kilocalories: 305

JEERA ALOO MATTAR

6 tablespoons sunflower oil
1 tablespoon white cumin seeds
2–4 cloves garlic, chopped finely
1 teaspoon Aromatic Salt (see page 8)
1 tablespoon Garam Masala (see page 10)
1 onion, sliced thinly
500 g (1 lb) mashed potato
250 g (8 oz) frozen peas, defrosted
TO GARNISH:
slices of red pepper
dill sprigs

Heat the oil in a frying pan or wok and stir-fry the cumin seeds for 1 minute. Add garlic to taste and stir-fry for 1 minute. Sprinkle with salt and garam masala. Add the onion and stir-fry for 3 minutes until it softens. Add the potato and peas and continue to stir-fry, combining the ingredients until heated through. Serve immediately, garnished with pepper slices and dill sprigs.

SERVES 4

Nutritional content per serving:	Carbohydrate: 35 g	Fat: 24 g	Fibre: 9 g	Kilocalories: 360

Potato Sallis; Spiced Roast Potatoes Makhanwalla; Jeera Aloo Mattar

SAG BHAJEE

750 g (1 ½ lb) spinach
2 tablespoons vegetable oil
1–4 cloves garlic, chopped
1 large onion, chopped
1 tablespoon Mild Curry Paste (see page 8)
salt
SPICES:
1 teaspoon white cumin seeds
1 teaspoon sesame seeds
1 teaspoon black mustard seeds*
½ teaspoon wild onion seeds* (optional)

If you are using fresh spinach, wash it in cold water very thoroughly to rid it of earth and grit. Chop the leaves coarsely and boil them for 5 minutes in just the water clinging to the leaves. Strain, discarding the water. Frozen spinach should be defrosted and drained and canned spinach drained of liquid. Heat the oil in a large frying pan or wok. Stir-fry the spices for 1 minute; add the garlic and stir-fry for 1 minute more; add the onion and stir-fry for 3 more minutes. Blend in the curry paste, bring the mixture to simmering point. Add the spinach and continue to cook, stirring frequently, until the spinach has heated through and the flavours have blended, about 5–7 minutes. Season with salt to taste and serve at once.

SERVES 4

Nutritional content per serving: Carbohydrate: 12 g   Fat: 10 g   Fibre: 2 g   Kilocalories: 160

MIXED VEGETABLE BHAJEE

ANY COMBINATION OF VEGETABLES CAN BE USED WITH THE CURRY BASE TO PRODUCE THIS BASIC BUT DELICIOUS VEGETABLE CURRY

750 g (1 ½ lb) mixed vegetables, e.g. 2 large
    potatoes, 2 carrots, 4 cauliflower florets,
    2 celery sticks, 4 broccoli florets, 5 baby
    sweetcorn cobs
3 tablespoons vegetable oil
300 ml (½ pint) Curry Purée (see page 9)
1 tablespoon Mild Curry Paste (see page 8)
3 tomatoes, sliced thinly
1 tablespoon chopped coriander*
2 teaspoons Garam Masala (see page 10)
salt
SPICES:
1 teaspoon white cumin seeds
1 teaspoon black mustard seeds*
¼ teaspoon coriander seeds*

Slice the vegetables into bite-sized pieces and blanch them. Drain, refresh in cold water and drain again if you wish to prepare the bhajee at a later stage, or use them hot straight away.

Heat the oil in a large frying pan or wok and stir-fry the spices for 1 minute. Add the curry purée and stir-fry for 5–6 minutes more. Mix in the curry paste and the tomatoes. When the mixture is bubbling, add the prepared vegetables, the chopped coriander and garam masala. Simmer until the vegetables are heated through and are as tender as you like. Season with salt to taste and serve at once.

SERVES 4

Nutritional content per serving:	Carbohydrate: 22 g	Fat: 19 g	Fibre: 4 g	Kilocalories: 250

MUSHROOM BHAJEE

VERY SMALL BUTTON MUSHROOMS ARE A FAVOURITE FOR THIS DISH. WIPE GENTLY WITH DAMP KITCHEN PAPER TO REMOVE DIRT AND GRIT. THEY NEED NO PRE-COOKING BUT ARE SIMPLY ADDED TO THE CURRY BASE BEFORE SERVING

3 tablespoons sunflower or mustard blend
    oil*
150 ml (¼ pint) Curry Purée (see page 9)
1 tablespoon chopped coriander*
2 teaspoons Garam Masala (see page 10)
1 tablespoon dried fenugreek*
Aromatic Salt (see page 8)
500 g (1 lb) button mushrooms, halved if
    large
SPICES:
1 teaspoon poppy seeds
1 teaspoon sesame seeds
1 teaspoon black mustard seeds*

Heat the oil in a 3 litre (5 pint) saucepan and stir-fry the spices for 1 minute. Add the curry purée and stir-fry for 3 minutes. Stir in the coriander, garam masala, fenugreek and aromatic salt to taste. Add the mushrooms, stir to coat them in the curry sauce and place the lid on the pan. Cook over a low heat for 10 minutes and serve at once.

Microwave: Place the oil in a large heatproof dish and cook on High Power for 2 minutes. Add the spices and cook on High Power for 2 minutes, stirring once. Add the curry purée and cook on High Power for 2 minutes, stirring once. Stir in the coriander, garam masala, fenugreek and aromatic salt to taste. Add the mushrooms and stir to coat, cover and cook on High Power for 6–8 minutes, stirring twice. Serve at once.

SERVES 4

Nutritional content per serving:	Carbohydrate: 3 g	Fat: 16 g	Fibre: 4 g	Kilocalories: 175

Sag Bhajee; Mixed Vegetables Bhajee; Mushroom Bhajee

NIRAMISH

WHICH VEGETABLES TO USE IS UP TO YOU; HERE I HAVE CHOSEN BABY SWEETCORN COBS, COURGETTES, MANGETOUT AND DWARF GREEN BEANS FOR A VARIETY OF COLOUR AND SHAPE AS WELL AS COMPLEMENTARY FLAVOURS

6 tablespoons vegetable oil
750 g (1½ lb) total weight mixed
　vegetables, e.g. 175 g (6 oz) baby
　sweetcorn cobs, 175 g (6 oz) courgettes,
　sliced, 175 g (6 oz) mangetout, whole,
　175 g (6 oz) dwarf green beans, topped
　and tailed
vegetable stock or water, to moisten
6–8 tablespoons lemon juice
1 tablespoon chopped coriander*
salt
SPICES:
2 teaspoons panch phoran* (optional)
½ teaspoon turmeric*
½–2 teaspoons chilli powder*

Heat the oil in a large frying pan or wok and stir-fry the spices for 1 minute. Add the vegetables and continue to stir-fry.

Cook them to taste – after 5 minutes they will be delightfully crisp; if you like them softer 10 minutes will be sufficient. Add a little vegetable stock or water if the vegetables become too dry.

Sprinkle over the lemon juice, coriander and salt to taste about 1 minute before serving.

Microwave: Place the oil in a large heatproof dish and cook on High Power for 3 minutes. Add the spices and cook on High Power for 2 minutes. Add the vegetables, cover and cook on High Power for 10 minutes, stirring twice. Sprinkle with lemon juice, coriander and salt to taste before serving.

SERVES 4

Nutritional content per serving:	Carbohydrate: 13 g	Fat: 23 g	Fibre: 4 g	Kilocalories: 270

BENGALI VEGETABLES

PANCH PHORAN*, THE BENGALI FIVE-SPICE MIXTURE, IS FRIED WITH ONION AND GARLIC BEFORE THE VEGETABLES OF YOUR CHOICE ARE ADDED. IN THIS CASE I HAVE USED SWEET POTATOES, WHICH ARE NOT IN FACT POTATOES AT ALL. THESE RED-SKINNED ROOT VEGETABLES ARE IDEAL SUBJECTS FOR SPICY COOKING

750 g (1½ lb) small sweet potatoes, peeled
　and chopped
6 tablespoons sunflower or mustard blend
　oil*
2 teaspoons panch phoran* spices or ½
　teaspoon white cumin seeds, ½ teaspoon
　fennel seeds, ½ teaspoon fenugreek
　seeds, ½ teaspoon black mustard seeds
　and ½ teaspoon wild onion seeds
2-4 cloves garlic, chopped
1 large onion, chopped
1 tablespoon chopped coriander*
salt

Boil the sweet potatoes until soft – about 15 minutes.

Meanwhile, heat the oil in a large frying pan or wok and stir-fry the panch phoran spices for 1 minute. Add the garlic and stir-fry for 1 minute more. Add the onion and stir-fry for 5 minutes more. As soon as the potatoes are ready, strain them and put them in the frying pan or wok with the chopped coriander. Stir-fry until the ingredients are well blended and heated through. Season with salt to taste and serve at once.

SERVES 4

Nutritional content per serving:	Carbohydrate: 40 g	Fat: 24 g	Fibre: 5 g	Kilocalories: 380

OKRA

ALSO KNOWN AS LADIES' FINGERS AND BHINDI, OKRA ARE A DELIGHTFUL AND TYPICALLY INDIAN VEGETABLE, USED IN MANY DISHES; CHOOSE SMALL OKRA FOR THE BEST RESULTS

4–6 tablespoons vegetable oil
2–4 cloves garlic, chopped finely
I large onion, sliced thinly
750 g (1½ lb) okra, topped and tailed
salt
3–4 tablespoons lemon juice
SPICES:
I teaspoon sesame seeds
2 tablespoons Mild Curry Powder
   (see page 7)

Heat the oil in a large frying pan or wok. Stir-fry the spices for 1 minute; add the garlic and stir-fry for 1 minute more. Add the onion and continue stir-frying for 5 more minutes. Add the okra and stir-fry for 5–6 minutes.

Season with salt to taste, sprinkle over the lemon juice and serve at once.

SERVES 4

Nutritional content per serving: Carbohydrate: 9 g   Fat: 16 g   Fibre: 7 g   Kilocalories: 200

Bengali Vegetables; Niramish; Okra

PANEER CURRY

PANEER IS THE CURDS MADE FROM FRESH MILK

PANEER:

2.4 litres (4 pints) pasteurized milk (not UHT)

4–6 tablespoons vinegar

vegetable oil for deep-frying

1 tablespoon chopped parsley to garnish

CURRY SAUCE:

2 tablespoons cornflour

whey (from the paneer making)

3 tablespoons sunflower oil

300 ml (½ pint) Curry Purée (see page 9)

1 tablespoon Mild Curry Paste (see page 8)

1 tablespoon tomato purée

250 g (8 oz) peas, fresh and lightly cooked or frozen and defrosted

salt

SPICES:

1 teaspoon white cumin seeds

1 teaspoon sesame seeds

1 teaspoon black mustard seeds*

First make the paneer. In a 5 litre (8 pint) saucepan, bring the milk to simmering point – it does not need to boil. Add the vinegar and stir vigorously. The curds will immediately separate from the whey. Keep stirring for 1–2 minutes and the whey will become clearer.

Line a large colander with a clean tea towel. Pour the curds and whey through, keeping the whey for use as stock. Fold the tea towel over the curds and lift it off the colander. Place it on the draining board and press down the curds inside the tea towel to make a circle 1–1.5 cm (½–¾ inch) thick. Put a heavy weight on top.

How long you leave it depends on the required texture of the paneer. If you want it crumbly like cottage cheese, leave it for 30 minutes–1 hour; remove the paneer from the tea towel, crumble it up with your fingers. If you want the paneer firm and close-textured, leave under the weight for 3–4 hours.

Remove the tea towel and cut the compressed curds into cubes. Before adding them to the sauce, deep-fry the cubes in oil heated to 190°C, 375°F for 10 minutes until they are golden like chips.

To make the sauce, mix the cornflour with enough whey to make a smooth paste. Heat the oil in a large frying pan or wok and stir-fry the spices for 1 minute. Add the curry purée and stir-fry for 5 more minutes. Add the cornflour paste and continue to stir-fry, gradually adding more whey as the sauce thickens, for 3 or 4 minutes more. Add the curry paste, tomato purée and peas and season with salt to taste. Mix the sauce well so that it has texture, adding a little more whey if you prefer a thinner consistency. Finally, add the crumbled paneer or fried paneer cubes and stir gently until the paneer is heated through – about 5 minutes. Garnish with chopped parsley and serve at once.

Microwave: Place the milk in a bowl and cook on High Power for 15–20 minutes or until very hot. Add the vinegar and prepare the paneer as above. Deep-fry as above. To make the sauce, mix the flour with enough whey to make a paste. Place the oil in a bowl and cook on High Power for 2 minutes. Add the spices and cook on High Power for 2 minutes. Add the curry purée and cook on High Power for 3 minutes, stirring once. Add the cornflour paste and cook on High Power for 2 minutes, stirring and gradually adding more whey as the sauce thickens. Add the curry paste, tomato purée and peas and season with salt. Add the cooked paneer and cook on High Power for 3–5 minutes, stirring gently twice, until the peas are cooked and the paneer is heated through.

SERVES 4

Nutritional content per serving: Carbohydrate: 40 g   Fat: 42 g   Fibre: 8 g   Kilocalories: 630

TOFU AND BURMESE BEAN SPROUTS

LIKE PANEER, TOFU IS AN EXCELLENT MEAT SUBSTITUTE, AND IN THIS TYPICALLY BURMESE RECIPE IT IS USED TO MAXIMUM EFFECT

250 g (8 oz) tofu (bean curd)

500 g (1 lb) bean sprouts

4 tablespoons vegetable oil

300 ml (½ pint) Curry Purée (see page 9)

1 tablespoon shrimp paste*, 1 tablespoon
   prawn ballichow* and 2
   tablespoons fish sauce* (nam pla), or 4
   tablespoons puréed anchovies

1 tablespoon desiccated coconut or
   coconut powder*

8 spring onions to garnish

Chop the tofu into 1 cm (½ inch) cubes and thoroughly wash the bean sprouts. Heat the oil in a large frying pan or wok. Stir-fry the curry purée for 5 minutes. Add the shrimp paste, prawn ballichow, fish sauce or puréed anchovies and coconut and mix them thoroughly into the purée. Bring the mixture to simmering point and add water little by little until it is the consistency you require – it should be quite thin. Add the bean sprouts and tofu to the sauce and bring it back to simmering point. To serve, garnish with the green leaves of the spring onions chopped into rings and the bulbs sliced vertically into quarters.

SERVES 4

Nutritional content per serving:	Carbohydrate: 7 g	Fat: 40 g	Fibre: 5 g	Kilocalories: 450

Paneer Curry; Tofu and Burmese Bean Sprouts

THAI VEGETABLE CURRY

FRAGRANT WATER:
175 ml (6 fl oz) water
4 tablespoons thinly pared lemon rind
GREEN PURÉE:
1 green pepper
1–6 green chillies*
1 bunch watercress
2 tablespoons chopped coriander*
4 spinach leaves
2–4 cloves garlic
5 cm (2 inch) piece fresh root ginger
CURRY:
4 tablespoons vegetable oil
2 puréed anchovies
2 tablespoons desiccated coconut
175 g (6 oz) can water chestnuts
475 g (15 oz) baby sweetcorn cobs
175 g (6 oz) bamboo shoots, sliced
TO GARNISH:
lime wedges
basil sprigs

Place the water in a saucepan with the lemon rind and boil for 1 minute. Remove from the heat and set aside for the flavour to infuse.

Place the ingredients for the green purée into a liquidizer and process until smooth, using a little water if necessary. Heat the oil in a large frying pan or wok and stir-fry the green purée for 5–6 minutes. Pour the fragrant water through a strainer and add the puréed anchovies and coconut mixed with water to a runny paste. Combine well to give a smooth mixture. Add the water chestnuts, baby sweetcorn cobs and bamboo shoots. If you are using canned vegetables, use some of their liquid for stock – enough to make the curry runny but not watery. Simmer the vegetables for 5–6 minutes. To serve, garnish with lime wedges and sprigs of basil.

SERVES 4

Nutritional content per serving: Carbohydrate: 11 g   Fat: 22 g   Fibre: 4 g   Kilocalories: 260

INDONESIAN VEGETABLE CURRY

SPICE PASTE:
2–6 cloves garlic
1 large onion, chopped finely
2.5cm (1 inch) piece fresh root ginger
1 red pepper, chopped
2–6 fresh red chillies*, chopped
10 unsalted cashew or candlenuts
1 teaspoon pepper
1 teaspoon turmeric*
CURRY:
4 tablespoons vegetable oil
3–4 tablespoons fresh lemon juice
300 g (10 oz) aubergines, chopped
300 g (10 oz) courgettes, sliced
1 head of Chinese leaves, bottom half only, chopped
1 tablespoon brown sugar
salt

Place all the ingredients for the spice paste into a blender and blend to a fairly stiff consistency, using as little water as possible. Heat the oil in a large frying pan or wok. Stir-fry the paste for 5 minutes, adding the lemon juice a little at a time, so that it is incorporated smoothly. Stir in enough water to make the sauce a pouring consistency. Add the aubergines, courgettes and Chinese leaves. Simmer for at least 5 or at most 10 minutes, until the aubergines are tender. Stir in the brown sugar and season with salt to taste. Serve at once.

SERVES 4

Nutritional content per serving: Carbohydrate: 17 g   Fat: 19 g   Fibre: 5 g   Kilocalories: 255

Burmese White Cabbage and Noodle Curry; Thai Vegetable Curry; Indonesian Vegetable Curry

BURMESE WHITE CABBAGE AND NOODLE CURRY

500 g (1 lb) white cabbage
3 tablespoons vegetable oil
2–4 cloves garlic, sliced thinly
1 teaspoon sesame seeds
1 teaspoon turmeric*
1 tablespoon chopped coriander*
6 spring onions, chopped finely
1–4 fresh green chillies*, chopped finely
1 red pepper, sliced thinly
200 g (7 oz) egg noodles
2 tablespoons fish sauce (nam pla)* or
    puréed anchovies
fresh coconut, shredded, or desiccated
    coconut to garnish (optional)

Shred the cabbage in a food processor or slice it very finely by hand. Heat the oil in a large frying pan or wok. Stir-fry the garlic for 1 minute; add the sesame seeds and turmeric and stir-fry for 1 minute longer. Add the coriander, spring onions, chillies and red pepper and bring the mixture to simmering point. Meanwhile, bring a large saucepan of water to the boil and place the noodles in it. When the water comes back to simmering point, remove the pan from the heat and leave it to stand for 8 minutes. Add the fish sauce or puréed anchovies and sliced cabbage to the frying pan or wok and cook briskly until the cabbage is tender but still retains some bite. Strain the noodles and add them to the vegetable mixture. To serve, garnish with coconut, if desired.

SERVES 4

Nutritional content per serving: Carbohydrate: 43 g   Fat: 17 g   Fibre: 7 g   Kilocalories: 360

DHAL

RED LENTILS (MASOOR DHAL) ARE SPECIFIED IN THIS RECIPE, BUT ANY OTHER TYPE OF LENTILS ARE SUITABLE

250 g (8 oz) red lentils
300 ml (½ pint) water
knob of concentrated butter or ghee*
salt
parsley sprigs to garnish
SPICES:
1 teaspoon garlic powder
1 teaspoon ground cumin
1 teaspoon Garam Masala (see page 10)

Rinse the lentils 2 or 3 times in cold water. Place them in a bowl with at least 3 times their volume of water and leave them to stand for 2–3 hours or overnight if necessary. Strain and rinse them again.

Bring the measured water to the boil. Add the lentils, stirring occasionally until they reach simmering point. Cover the saucepan and cook for 20 minutes. The lentils should have absorbed the water, but will not yet be cooked.

Add the spices and simmer the dhal for 10–15 minutes more, stirring occasionally to prevent it sticking. Stir in the butter or ghee and season with salt to taste. Serve immediately, garnished with parsley sprigs.

SERVES 4 as an accompaniment

Nutritional content per serving: Carbohydrate: 34 g   Fat: 4 g   Fibre: 8 g   Kilocalories: 225

RAJMA LOBIA CURRY

THIS DISH COMBINES RED KIDNEY BEANS (RAJMA) AND BLACK-EYED BEANS (LOBIA) IN A SPICY CURRY BASE. TO SAVE TIME, CANNED BEANS MAY BE USED, WITH THEIR LIQUID, INSTEAD OF THE DRIED BEANS

250 g (8 oz) red kidney beans
250 g (8 oz) black-eyed beans
3 tablespoons vegetable oil
40 g (1½ oz) fresh root ginger, sliced thinly
1 onion, chopped
300 ml (½ pint) tomato juice or tomato
   soup
salt
3–4 tablespoons lemon or lime juice
chervil sprigs to garnish
SPICES:
2 teaspoons Garam Masala (see page 10)
1 teaspoon ground coriander*
1 teaspoon ground cumin
½ teaspoon chilli powder*

Rinse the kidney beans in cold water and drain. Place them in a bowl with twice their volume of cold water and leave to soak overnight.

Next day rinse the beans in cold water 3 or 4 times. Follow the same procedure of rinsing and soaking for the black-eyed beans, keeping them separate from the kidney beans. Take 2 saucepans and place 1.2 litres (2 pints) of water in each. Bring each to the boil. Put the kidney beans in one pan and the black-eyed beans in the other and rapidly boil them both for 45 minutes.

After about 30 minutes heat the oil in a large frying pan or wok and stir-fry the ginger for 1 minute. Add the onion and continue to stir-fry for 3 or 4 minutes. Quickly mix the spices with enough water to make a paste. Add the paste to the frying pan or wok and stir it in for 2–3 minutes. Add the tomato juice or soup and cook until it comes to simmering point. As soon as the beans are tender and completely cooked, strain them and add them to the pan. Season with salt to taste, and stir in fresh lemon or lime juice just before serving. Garnish with chervil sprigs.

SERVES 4

Nutritional content per serving: Carbohydrate: 64 g   Fat: 15 g   Fibre: 33 g   Kilocalories: 480

Dhal; Rajma Lobia Curry; Tarka Channa Dhal

TARKA CHANNA DHAL

TO SAVE TIME, THE SAME QUANTITY OF CANNED CHICK PEAS MAY BE USED IN THIS DISH

50 g (2 oz) chick peas
175 g (6 oz) red lentils
2 tablespoons oil
2–4 cloves garlic, chopped finely
1 large onion, sliced thinly
1 tablespoon Mild Curry Paste (see page 8)
salt
parsley sprigs to garnish
SPICES:
2 teaspoons white cumin seeds
2 teaspoons black mustard seeds*

Rinse the chick peas and lentils separately 2 or 3 times. Still keeping them separate, soak them in plenty of cold water overnight to allow them to swell and soften.

Drain the chick peas. Boil 1.2 litres (2 pints) of water in a saucepan and boil the chick peas vigorously for 45 minutes. Drain the red lentils and in another pan bring 450 ml (¾ pint) water to the boil. Add the lentils and bring the water back to simmering point, stirring from time to time. Cover the pan and leave to simmer for 20 minutes. Stir the lentils to prevent them sticking to the pan. Add a little water if necessary and continue to simmer. Meanwhile, heat the oil in a large frying pan or wok. Stir-fry the spices for 1 minute. Add the garlic and stir-fry for 1 minute more. Add the onion and stir-fry for 5 minutes more. Blend in the curry paste. When the mixture is smooth take the pan off the heat. Taste the chick peas and lentils to make sure they are cooked. Strain the chick peas and add them to the red lentils. Add the fried mixture to the dhal and season with salt to taste. Transfer to a heated dish and serve hot, garnished with parsley sprigs.

SERVES 4

Nutritional content per serving:	Carbohydrate: 34 g	Fat: 10 g	Fibre: 8 g	Kilocalories: 270

EKOORI

THIS DISH FROM THE BOMBAY PARSEES ADDS ZEST TO CONVENTIONAL SCRAMBLED EGG

knob of concentrated butter or
   ghee*
1 clove garlic, chopped finely
6 eggs, lightly beaten
Aromatic Salt (see page 8)
SPICES:
1 teaspoon white cumin seeds
1 teaspoon sesame seeds
½ teaspoon turmeric*
TO GARNISH:
Garam Masala (see page 10)

Heat the butter or ghee in a small saucepan. Stir-fry the spices for 1 minute; add the garlic and stir-fry for 1 minute more. Add the eggs and keep stirring over a low to moderate heat until the eggs have reached the texture you prefer. Sprinkle with aromatic salt to taste.

Transfer to heated individual plates. Serve immediately, garnished with garam masala, and accompanied with Chupatti, Puri (see pages 92 or 93) or toast.

SERVES 4 as a snack

Nutritional content per serving: Carbohydrate: 2 g   Fat: 12 g   Kilocalories: 150

QUAIL'S EGG CURRY

QUAIL'S EGGS ARE PARTICULARLY ATTRACTIVE IN APPEARANCE AND TASTE, BUT SUBSTITUTE 8 HEN'S EGGS 'IF'YOU PREFER

24 quail's eggs
2 tablespoons oil
300 ml (½ pint) Curry Purée (see page 9)
2 tablespoons Mild Curry Paste (see page 8)
1 × 425 g (14 oz) can chopped tomatoes
1 tablespoon dried fenugreek leaves*
2 teaspoon dried mint
1 tablespoon desiccated coconut or
    coconut powder*
2 tablespoons single cream
1 tablespoon Garam Masala (see page 10)
salt
mint sprigs to garnish

Prick the blunt end of each egg with a pin, just piercing the shell into the sac of air. (This will prevent the eggs from cracking when placed in boiling water. It also helps if they are at room temperature.) Boil 1.2 litres (2 pints) of water in a large saucepan. Carefully lower the eggs into the boiling water and let them boil for a total of 4 minutes.

Remove the pan from the heat and immediately run cold water into it to cool the eggs and stop them cooking further. Shell the eggs and let them stand in cold water while making the curry sauce.

Heat the oil in a large frying pan or wok and stir-fry the curry purée for 5 minutes. Add the curry paste, tomatoes, fenugreek and mint. Bring the mixture to simmering point, and stir in the coconut, cream and garam masala. Season with salt to taste, and add water if necessary to obtain a creamy consistency. Bring the sauce back to simmering point and carefully add the eggs. Let the curry cook for 5 minutes to heat the eggs through and serve immediately, garnished with mint sprigs.

SERVES 4

Nutritional content per serving: Carbohydrate: 7 g   Fat: 33 g   Fibre: 2 g   Kilocalories: 375

PERSIAN OMELETTE

THIS OMELETTE IS DELIGHTFUL IN ITS OWN RIGHT BUT CAN ALSO BE SERVED WITH OTHER DISHES. THIS RECIPE MAKES ENOUGH FOR TWO PEOPLE; FOR FOUR, MAKE A SECOND OMELETTE, KEEPING THE FIRST ONE WARM

2 teaspoons chopped coriander*
2 teaspoons chopped parsley
1 teaspoon snipped chives
1 teaspoon chopped mixed herbs
1–3 green chillies*, chopped (optional)
4 eggs
1 tablespoon concentrated butter or ghee*
TO GARNISH:
Aromatic Salt (see page 8)
Garam Masala (see page 10)
Mild Curry Powder (see page 7)
parsley sprigs

Combine the chopped herbs with the chillies, if using. Break the eggs into a large bowl and gently whisk them with a fork, mixing in the herbs. Let this mixture stand for 30 minutes.

Heat a 25 cm (10 inch) frying pan. When the pan is hot, put in the butter or ghee. Let it melt and swirl it around to cover the surface of the pan. Give the egg mixture a final stir and tip it into the pan, swirling it around to cover the whole pan. Spread it out with the fork. Shake the pan to prevent the omelette from sticking. When it is set enough for your taste fold it into 3 and cut it in half.

Transfer to individual heated plates and serve immediately, sprinkled with aromatic salt, garam masala, curry powder and parsley sprigs.

SERVES 2

Nutritional content per serving: Fibre: 2 g   Fat: 17 g   Kilocalories: 210

Quail's Egg Curry; Ekoori; Persian Omelette

ACCOMPANIMENTS

THE STAPLES THAT TRADITIONALLY ACCOMPANY CURRY ARE EITHER FLAT ROUND WHEAT FLOUR BREADS OR PLAIN OR AROMATIC RICE OR BOTH, AND NO CURRY DISH IS COMPLETE WITHOUT A SELECTION OF FRESH CHUTNEYS AND PICKLES EACH OF WHICH HAS A DISTINCTIVE FLAVOUR.

PULLAO RICE

AROMATIC SPICES ARE FRIED INTO THE BASMATI RICE AND COCONUT AND GROUND ALMONDS ARE ADDED AFTER BOILING. USE ALL OR A MIXTURE OF ANY OF THE SPICES LISTED BELOW

300 g (10 oz) Basmati rice
1 tablespoon concentrated butter or ghee*
1 tablespoon ground almonds
1 tablespoon desiccated coconut or
  coconut powder*
20 strands saffron* (optional)
SPICES:
½ teaspoon fennel seeds*
½ teaspoon black cumin seeds
4 green cardamoms*
4 whole cloves
2 star anise*
2.5cm (1 inch) piece cinnamon stick or
  cassia bark*

Leave the rice to soak for about 30 minutes in cold water.

Bring 1.8 litres (3 pints) of water to the boil. Give the rice several rinses in cold water then a final rinse with hot water. Tip the rice into the saucepan, put on the lid and start timing precisely. After 1 minute give the rice a stir and replace the lid. After 6 minutes taste a few grains: the rice should be almost cooked. Simmer for 1–2 minutes more. Strain off all the excess water. The rice can be left to go cold or used at once.

Heat the butter or ghee in a large frying pan or wok and fry the spices for 1 minute. Add the rice and stir-fry until it has reached serving temperature. Add the ground almonds, coconut and saffron, if using.

Transfer the rice to a lidded serving bowl and keep it warm until you are ready to serve. Before serving fluff up the rice with a fork from time to time to allow any steam to escape.

SERVES 4

Nutritional content per serving: Carbohydrate: 68 g   Fat: 9 g   Fibre: 4 g   Kilocalories: 350

LIME RICE

300 g (10 oz) Basmati rice
600 ml (1 pint) water
2 tablespoons sunflower or mustard blend
  oil*
2 tablespoons unsalted cashew nuts
flesh of ¼ coconut, grated or 1 tablespoon
  desiccated coconut
3–4 tablespoons lime juice
SPICES:
1 teaspoon black mustard seeds*
1 teaspoon sesame seeds
1 teaspoon crushed dried curry leaves*
  (optional)
½ teaspoon turmeric*
½ teaspoon mango powder* (optional)

Leave the rice to soak for about 30 minutes in cold water.

In a 3 litre (5 pint) flameproof lidded casserole bring the water to the boil. Rinse the rice 2 or 3 times in cold water, then finally in hot water. Tip the rice into the casserole and stir from time to time until the water returns to the boil. Place the lid on the casserole and turn the heat down to low. Let the rice cook for 8 minutes.

Meanwhile heat the oil in a frying pan and fry the cashew nuts for 2 minutes; add the spices and fry them for 1 minute. Stir the oil, nuts and spices into the rice.

Add the coconut and lime juice and place the casserole into a preheated oven, 110°C, 225°F, Gas Mark ¼ (the lowest setting) for a minimum of 30 minutes. It can be kept warm for 1–2 hours without spoiling. Just before serving, fluff up the rice with a fork to allow any steam to escape.

SERVES 4

Nutritional content per serving: Carbohydrate: 69 g   Fat: 14 g   Fibre: 3 g   Kilocalories: 410

Pullao Rice; Lime Rice

CHUPPATI

THE CHUPPATI IS AN UNLEAVENED DISC ABOUT 15 CM (6 INCHES) IN DIAMETER, MADE FROM FINE-GROUND HARD WHOLEMEAL FLOUR (ATA FLOUR*) AND DRY-COOKED. THESE ARE EASY TO MAKE AND ENHANCE ANY CURRY MEAL

500 g (1 lb) ata* or wholemeal flour
warm water
Aromatic Salt (see page 8)

Mix the flour with enough water to make a soft pliable dough. Let it stand for about 30 minutes.

Divide the dough into 8 pieces. Roll each piece out to a circle about 18–20 cm (7–8 inches) in diameter.

Heat a large heavy frying pan over a fairly high heat. Place the chuppatis on the dry pan one at a time. After 20–30 seconds characteristic dark patches appear, which look appetizing and taste good.

Turn the chuppati over and cook the other side for about 30 seconds. Sprinkle with aromatic salt. Serve promptly or they cool and harden.

SERVES 8

Nutritional content per serving: Carbohydrate: 80 g   Fat: 1 g   Fibre: 6 g   Kilocalories: 200

PUPPADOMS

IT TAKES A LIFETIME OF EXPERIENCE PLUS ABOUT TEN DAYS OF CONSTANT HIGH TEMPERATURES AND SUNLIGHT TO PRODUCE A PUPPADOM – THAT THIN CIRCULAR WAFER WHICH PRECEDES THE INDIAN MEAL. WHICHEVER METHOD OF COOKING YOU USE, REMEMBER THAT PUPPADOMS CAN BE COOKED IN ADVANCE OF EATING AND STAY CRISP FOR HOURS ESPECIALLY IF KEPT IN A WARM PLACE

1 packet ready-to-cook plain or spicy puppadoms

For a dry, lightly bubbled effect, place 2 puppadoms on the grill pan positioned at the half-way point under a preheated hot grill. They will cook in under 10 seconds so keep a constant watch on them so that they do not burn. Turn them once and cook the other side for a few seconds to make sure they are completely cooked.

A richer, more even effect (and much higher in calories) is achieved by deep-frying 1 puppadom at a time in oil preheated to 190°C, 375°C. Using tongs, immerse the puppadom in the oil. It will sizzle and enlarge, and be fully cooked in about 15 seconds. Remove, shake off excess oil and stand on its edge on kitchen paper to drain.

Microwave: Place up to a maximum of 3 plain or spicy puppadoms on the base of the microwave or turntable so that they do not overlap or touch. Cook on High Power until bubbling and puffy. One puppadom will take 20–25 seconds to cook and 2–3 will take about 45–60 seconds to cook. Carefully remove the puppadoms from the microwave and leave to stand on a wire rack for 15 seconds to crisp. The benefit of cooking these in a microwave is that no extra oil is required and there is no need for constant attention.

Nutritional content per puppadom: Carbohydrate: 7 g   Fibre: 2 g   Kilocalories: 40

PURI

LIKE CHUPPATIS, PURIS ARE MADE WITH ATA FLOUR* BUT PURIS ARE ONLY 10 CM (4 INCHES) ACROSS AND THEY ARE DEEP-FRIED

225 g (8 oz) ata* or wholemeal flour
1 tablespoon concentrated butter or ghee*
250 ml (8 fl oz) warm water
vegetable oil for deep-frying
Aromatic Salt (see page 8)

Mix the flour, butter or ghee and water into a soft dough and let it stand for about 30 minutes to become soft. Divide the dough into 16 pieces. Shape each one into a ball and roll them out to make 10 cm (4 inch) discs. Deep-fry the puris one at a time in oil preheated to 190°C, 375°F for 20 seconds or until they puff up like balloons. Remove each one from the oil as soon as it is ready, sprinkle with aromatic salt and serve at once.

SERVES 8

Nutritional content per serving: Carbohydrate: 9 g   Fat: 7 g   Fibre: 2 g   Kilocalories: 110

Chuppati; Puri; Puppadoms

CUCUMBER RAITA

YOGURT, CREAM AND LIGHT SPICES MAKE RAITA, INTO WHICH ONE CAN ADD VEGETABLES SUCH AS CUCUMBER. RAITAS ARE PARTICULARLY MILD AND SOOTHING – A GOOD ANTIDOTE FOR A CURRY WHICH YOU FIND TOO HOT

5 cm (2 inch) piece cucumber
6 tablespoons natural yogurt
2 tablespoons double cream
1 teaspoon Garam Masala (see page 10)
paprika to garnish

Cut the cucumber into julienne strips (matchstick shapes). Combine the cucumber with the yogurt, cream and garam masala and place the raita in a serving dish.

Sprinkle with paprika and chill briefly before serving.

SERVES 4–6

Nutritional content per serving:	Carbohydrate: 3 g	Fat: 4 g	Kilocalories: 50

FRESH CHILLI

A VIBRANT, VERY HOT CHUTNEY WHICH IS NOT FOR THE NOVICE. AS IT KEEPS VERY WELL, IT IS WORTH MAKING ENOUGH FOR SEVERAL MEALS, WHICH WILL BE PROVIDED BY THE AMOUNTS GIVEN IN THIS RECIPE

250 g (8 oz) fresh green chillies*
250 ml (8 fl oz) vinegar

Place the chillies in a blender or food processor with the vinegar and work to a purée.

Place the purée in a sterilized jar. Top up the jar with vinegar to prevent a mould from forming. Cover the jar tightly.

The chutney will change from bright to dark green in colour after 1–2 weeks but will keep indefinitely.

MAKES APPROXIMATELY 250 g (8 oz)

Nutritional content per quantity:	Carbohydrate: 25 g	Fat: 4 g	Fibre: 3 g	Kilocalories: 290

MINT RAITA

FRESH MINT IS ADDED TO THE BASIC YOGURT AND CREAM COMBINATION. THIS RAITA USUALLY ACCOMPANIES TANDOORI DISHES

2 tablespoons finely chopped mint leaves
6 tablespoons natural yogurt
1 tablespoon double cream
1 teaspoon Garam Masala (see page 10)
mint sprigs to garnish

Mix the mint with the yogurt, cream and garam masala. Place the raita in a serving bowl.

Chill briefly before serving garnished with mint sprigs.

SERVES 4–6

Nutritional content per serving:	Carbohydrate: 2 g	Fat: 2 g	Fibre: 1 g	Kilocalories: 35

Cucumber Raita; Fresh Chilli; Mint Raita; Cachumber